902816661 0

Please return/renew this item by the last date shown.
Items may also be renewed by the internet*

https://library.eastriding.gov.uk

* Please note a PIN will be required to access this service
- this c~~ ~~ ~~~~~~~~ from your library

D1407478

Please Note

Although every care has been taken with the production of this book to ensure that all information is correct at the time of writing and that any projects, designs, modifications and/ or programs, etc., contained herewith, operate in a correct and safe manner and also that any components specified are normally available in Great Britain, the Publishers and Author do not accept responsibility in any way for the failure (including fault in design) of any project, design, modification or program to work correctly or to cause damage to any equipment that it may be connected to or used in conjunction with, or in respect of any other damage or injury that may be so caused, nor do the Publishers accept responsibility in any way for the failure to obtain specified components.

Notice is also given that if equipment that is still under warranty is modified in any way or used or connected with home-built equipment then that warranty may be void.

© 2017 BERNARD BABANI (publishing) LTD

First Published – October 2017

British Library Cataloguing in Publication Data:

A catalogue record for this book is available from the British Library

ISBN 978-0-85934-771-6

Cover Design by Gregor Arthur

Printed and bound in Great Britain for Bernard Babani (publishing) Ltd

About this Book

The BBC micro:bit is a "computer on a chip" - a microcomputer smaller than a credit card. It is part of a major international project to help students enjoy learning about computers and stimulate their interest in technology.

Python is a computer programming language widely used in education, business and other organisations because it's powerful yet easy to learn. This book is based on MicroPython, a version of Python 3 which has been implemented on the micro:bit by Damien P. George. The main features of the Python language and programming in general are covered, so the material is very relevant to anyone wishing to follow a career in computing.

This book shows how to write programs for the micro:bit to create and display text messages and images on its array of 25 LEDs. Also to connect a speaker or headphones and create and play music, sounds and synthesised speech.

Exercises to re-inforce coding skills are given throughout the book. These include the use of the micro:bit's accelerometer to detect movement — very relevant in today's digital world for the control and navigation of ships, aircraft, cars and the prevention of accidents involving domestic appliances.

Also included is a comprehensive glossary of computer terms and a detailed explanation of the various levels of language used to communicate with computers.

This book is intended to help beginners of all ages to enjoy learning Python programming, whether as a pupil (or parent) as part of the school curriculum, a student of any age considering a career in computing or an enthusiast, coding in Python as an enjoyable and stimulating hobby.

About the Author

Jim Gatenby trained as a Chartered Engineer and initially worked at Rolls-Royce Ltd., using computers in the analysis of jet engine performance. He obtained a Master of Philosophy degree in Mathematical Education and taught mathematics and computing for 24 years to students of all ages and abilities, in school and in adult education. This work involved the BBC Model B computer of which the ARM processor used in the BBC micro:bit is a descendant.

The author has written over fifty books in the fields of GCSE Computer Studies, programming in BBC BASIC, Microsoft Windows and Office, and Android tablets and smartphones, all of which have been very well received.

Trademarks

Python is a trademark or registered trademark of the Python Software Foundation. All other brand and product names used in this book are recognized as trademarks or registered trademarks of their respective companies.

Acknowledgements

I would like to thank Damien P. George and Nicholas H. Tollervey, creators of MicroPython and the Mu MicroPython Editor respectively, and major contributors to the BBC micro:bit project. Much of this book draws on their original work, without which the book would not have been possible. Also for their help and support when I initially approached them for permission to write this book.

I would also like to thank my wife Jill and my publisher Michael Babani for their continued support throughout this project.

Contents

3

4

5

6

Python Skills are Valuable and Transferable

The Python/MicroPython programming language covered in this book is very popular in primary, secondary and university education, as well as organisations such as Google, NASA and IBM. Also many of the statements, keywords and rules of Python are very similar to those in other popular programming languages such as Java and C.

For example, important Python keywords discussed in this book and used in other programming languages include break, if, else, for, in, false, true and while.

So time spent acquiring Python skills will also be helpful in learning other very popular programming languages such as C, C++, Java and JavaScript.

Introduction

The BBC micro:bit Project

This is a major project designed to help young people learn about computers and write their own *code*, also known as *programs*. Programs are instructions written in a special language based on English, telling the computer what to do.

The micro:bit project is also intended to help Britain compete in a world which increasingly relies on computers.

This book covers two important aspects of the project:

- The BBC micro:bit itself.
- The MicroPython programming language, discussed shortly.

The BBC micro:bit

The micro:bit is a small electronic circuit board as shown below. It's also a computer capable of performing some of the functions carried out by much larger machines.

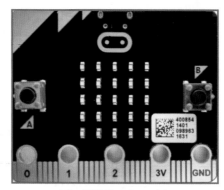

The BBC micro:bit

The micro:bit is a type of *microcontroller*, also known as a *System On a Chip* or *SOC*. An *embedded system* is a microcontroller built into other devices such as:

- Domestic appliances
- Smartphones
- Cars, other vehicles and robots
- Security alarms
- Cash points and vending machines

In 2016 approximately 1 million children in year 7 in UK schools were provided with free micro:bits. The micro:bit is now also available to buy over-the-counter, so for around £15 you can learn about the basics of computing, either as a fascinating hobby or as a stepping stone to a new career.

The micro:bit project has now gone global, thanks to the formation of the *Micro:bit Educational Foundation*, a non-profit organisation supported by companies and organisations such as the BBC, the Python Software Partnership, Microsoft, ARM, Amazon, Barclays Bank, Lancaster University and Samsung.

There is also a very large *micro:bit developer community* supported by volunteers who help to co-ordinate the project and share their computing expertise by developing software and learning materials.

These include Nicholas Tollervey, who created the popular *Mu* and Web browser *editors* for writing your own programs. Also Damien George, who created MicroPython, a version of the Python 3 programming language adapted for very small microcomputers such as the BBC micro:bit and the *pyboard*, which he developed.

The Anatomy of the BBC micro:bit

The micro:bit contains all the main components of a computer system, as shown below on the micro:bit front view and on the rear view on page 4. These include:

- A *memory*, where *programs* or sets of instructions are stored. The memory also stores the *data* for a program, such as names, text and images.
- A *processor* which can *run* or *execute* a program.
- *Input* devices. These include a *micro-USB port* (shown on the next page) allowing programs to be transferred to the micro:bit from other computers.
- *Output* devices including an array or matrix of *LEDs* (Light Emitting Diodes) enabling text and images to be displayed, scrolled and animated.
- Various *connectors* (outlined in yellow below), allowing devices such as speakers to be attached.
- *Buttons A* and *B* which can be programmed to initiate various actions when pressed.

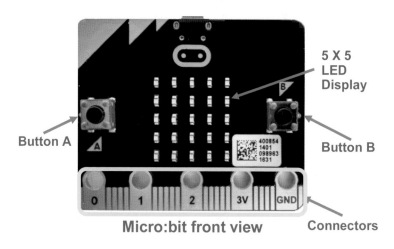

Micro:bit front view

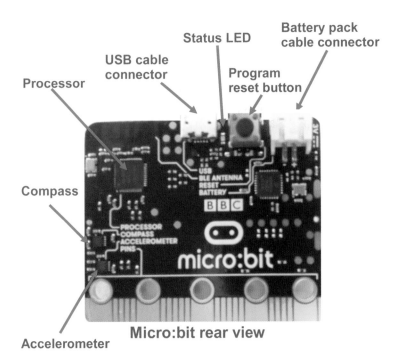

Micro:bit rear view

Components on the rear of the micro:bit shown above include:

- An *accelerometer* to sense movement of the micro:bit and a *compass* to measure direction. So, for example, the micro:bit can be used to control the movement of mobile devices such as a buggy or a robot.

- As shown above, there is a *program reset button*. This restarts and runs the program currently in the micro:bit's memory.

- The *Status* or *System LED* is located on the back of the micro:bit, as shown above. This flashes when a program is being copied to the micro:bit from another device.

Powering the micro:bit

USB cable

Obviously the micro:bit doesn't have it's own keyboard and screen for typing in your *programs*, so this is done on larger computers, laptops, tablets, etc. Then the programs are copied or "flashed" to the memory of the micro:bit where they are executed or run automatically. On PC machines and laptops the connection is made using a USB cable, shown on the left below. The USB cable also delivers power from the computer to the micro:bit.

Battery pack

It's also possible to use the micro:bit when it's not connected to another computer by a USB cable. For example, to run a program already stored in the memory of the micro:bit. In this case the micro:bit can be powered by a plug-in battery pack, containing two AAA 1.5V batteries as shown below.

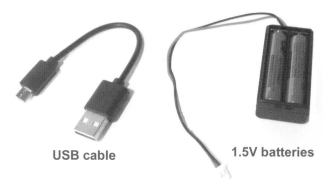

USB cable   1.5V batteries

The above accessories can be bought separately or as part of a BBC micro:bit kit, from suppliers such as Maplin, Kitronik, Farnell and Amazon. Many other accessories are available for the micro:bit, together with ideas for projects and learning and teaching materials.

Programming the BBC micro:bit

Programs, also known as *source code*, are step-by-step instructions or *statements* telling the computer what to do. Statements are written in special languages which use English words, but within their own strict rules or *syntax*. This book is based on MicroPython, a version of the popular Python 3 programming language. Python was created by Guido van Rossum and is designed to be easy to use with lots of indentation and white space separating blocks of code.

Python was chosen for this book because:

- Python is powerful yet easy to learn.

- Python is widely used in large organisations, business and education. Well-known users include Google, Yahoo!, IBM and NASA.

- The Mu editor and the browser editor make it very easy for beginners to write their own MicroPython programs.

- MicroPython is already an integral part of the BBC micro:bit, built in as standard.

MicroPython was written by Damien George for use on the *pyboard*, which he created, and also the BBC micro:bit. MicroPython is a slimmed down version of the original Python 3 language designed for much larger computers.

Writing programs in MicroPython is essentially the same as programming in Python 3. So skills acquired by learning MicroPython for the micro:bit are directly transferable to programming in Python 3 in the wider world of education, commerce and industry.

Algorithms and Programs

An algorithm is a step-by-step plan for a program, in plain English. Shown below is an algorithm for a program to scroll the message "Hi, Everyone" ten times, lighting up the 5 x 5 LED matrix on the front of the micro-bit.

> Set a counter to 1
> While the counter is less than 11
> Display and scroll "Hi, Everyone"
> Add 1 to the counter
> Wait a short time

A short algorithm

This is coded in the more structured Python language as shown below. Don't worry if you don't understand it — this Python source code is explained in detail later.

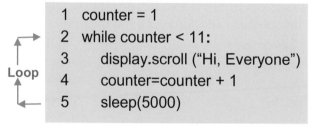

```
1   counter = 1
2   while counter < 11:
3       display.scroll ("Hi, Everyone")
4       counter=counter + 1
5       sleep(5000)
```

Loop

A Python program

The small example above is just to show that a program consists of lines of English words and numbers, laid out in a structured format with rules for spacing and punctuation. Words such as while and display are *keywords* or *reserved* words with special meanings in the MicroPython language.

High Level Languages

A computer, being an electronic device, is a *two-state system*. At its centre, a computer represents numbers, letters, instructions and data using millions of tiny switches.

These are either ON or OFF and are used to represent the numbers 0 and 1, known as *binary digits* (*bits* for short). So at its lowest level, everything in a computer such as names, numbers and instructions are coded in patterns of 0s and 1s.

Long groups of binary digits are too unwieldy for humans to work with. So computer scientists invented *high-level* languages such as Python, using English words to represent the instructions and data in a program.

These instructions in a high-level language are then translated into the machine's own language, known as *machine code*, by a program called a *compiler*. The compiler creates a complete, standalone machine code program which doesn't need to be translated again each time you run or execute the program. Another type of translation program, called an *interpreter*, is used in some situations. The interpreter translates a script in a high-level language line by line every time you run the program.

Machine code is basically long strings of 0's and 1's, but for simplicity these are usually displayed in *hexadecimal format (.hex)*, which represents each group of four binary digits (known as 1 *nibble*) using the 16 .hex codes 0-9 and A-F.

So the finished program in the Python language is converted to a hexadecimal file (.hex) before it can be run or executed in the BBC micro:bit.

You can start programming the micro:bit using Python without being an expert on binary, machine code and hexadecimal. However, if you need to know more, these topics are covered in more detail in Appendix 1.

Executing Programs on the BBC mico:bit

The main steps in creating and running a MicroPython program on the BBC micro:bit are as follows:

- If necessary, write an *algorithm* or list of steps for the task, in plain English.
- Using a laptop or desktop computer, write the *source code* in MicroPython, using either the Mu editor or the Web browser editor, discussed shortly.
- Connect the computer to the micro:bit using a USB cable.
- Copy or *flash* the program to the micro:bit using a USB cable connection.
- The program runs automatically on the micro:bit as soon as copying is complete.

Memory on the micro:bit

The micro:bit has *flash memory*, like removable flash drives or memory sticks used for storage on laptop and desktop computers. This means a program stays in the memory of the micro:bit until it's overwritten by a new program. The current program will also run every time you plug the micro:bit into a power supply such as a USB computer connection or a battery pack.

The flash memory on the BBC micro:bit has a storage capacity of 256KB (Kilobytes). 1byte is the amount of storage space needed to hold one character such as a letter of the alphabet or a digit in the range 0 to 9. 1Kilobyte is 1024bytes. Bits, bytes and kilobytes, etc., are covered in more detail in Appendix 1.

Summary

- The BBC micro:bit is part of a major educational initiative supported by several large organisations. Initially a UK project, it is now a worldwide scheme.

- The BBC micro:bit is a *micro computer* and *microcontroller*. It is powered by connecting it to another computer using a *USB cable* or by a *battery pack*.

- Numerous *connectors* allow external devices such as speakers and robots to be attached to the micro:bit.

- The micro:bit can be programmed to display text, images and animations on a grid of *LEDs*, play music and games and detect movement and direction.

- Programs, i.e. sets of instructions, for the micro:bit are written using a separate computer.

- Also known as *source code* or scripts, programs are written in a high level language using English words.

- The source code is translated into *hexadecimal code (.hex)* by a program called a *compiler*. Hexadecimal is very close to the actual binary machine code (0's and 1's) used inside the computer.

- The hexadecimal file is copied to the *flash memory* of the micro:bit using a USB cable.

- The micro:bit can be programmed using a variety of high level languages. This book uses *BBC micro:bit MicroPython*, a version of the Python 3 language.

- Python is easy to learn and popular in education and commerce. So there should be good employment opportunities for Python programmers.

2

Introducing the
Browser Editor

Introduction

A program called a *source code editor* is used to type the statements of your own program on the screen. The editor helps you lay out the program with line numbers and spacing as required by the MicroPython programming language. As its name implies, the editor also allows you to correct mistakes and add extra lines to develop a program.

There are two basic approaches to writing and editing MicroPython programs for the BBC micro:bit.

- Using the *microbit.org Web site* which has a built-in MicroPython editor running in your *Web browser*.

- Installing the *Mu* MicroPython editor which is downloaded and saved on your computer.

Both of the MicroPython editors above were themselves written in the Python language by Nicholas Tollervey and have been designed to be easy for beginners to use.

The next few pages describe how to start using the browser editor on a laptop or desktop PC, at the official Web site:

http://microbit.org

Chapter 3 describes how to install the Mu editor software and use it to create and run MicroPython programs on the BBC micro:bit.

Using the Browser Editor

The Web site editor can be accessed directly through your Web browser such as Microsoft Edge or Internet Explorer on PCs or Safari on Mac computers. You will also need a USB cable to connect the computer to the micro:bit.

Enter **http://microbit.org** into your browser and select **Let's Code** as shown below.

Scroll down the screen and under Python Editor select **Let's Code** again.

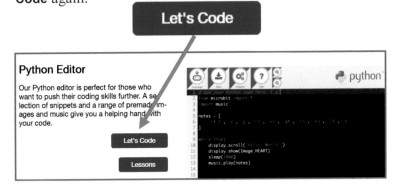

The browser editor opens as shown on the next page. It already has a sample program entered. It's traditional for beginners to start with a program to display the message **'Hello, World!'** on the computer screen or in this case the array of 5 x 5 LEDs on the micro:bit.

Create a Shortcut
To save typing the address **http://microbit.org** every time you want to do some coding, you may wish to create a *desktop icon* or alternatively a *favourite* for the Web site.

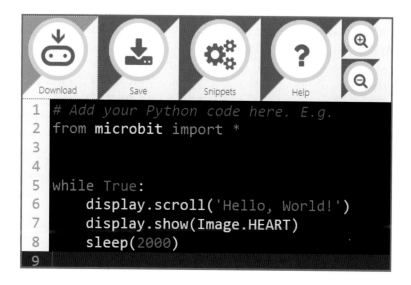

```
1  # Add your Python code here. E.g.
2  from microbit import *
3
4
5  while True:
6      display.scroll('Hello, World!')
7      display.show(Image.HEART)
8      sleep(2000)
9
```

The lines of code which make up a MicroPython program like the one above are discussed in detail in the Chapter 4.

The next section describes the method of running or executing this program on the BBC micro:bit.

The main steps are:

- Download the code from the Internet browser on to your computer (laptop or desktop, etc.)

- Save the program as a .hex file on your computer's hard drive.

- Connect the micro:bit to your computer.

- Copy the .hex file to the micro:bit.

- The program is saved on the micro:bit and runs automatically.

Copying a Program to the micro:bit
(From the Web browser Editor)

Writing your own programs is discussed in detail in the rest of this book. This section explains how to copy a program from the browser editor and run it on the micro:bit.

We will now take the sample **'Hello, World!'** code and copy it to the micro:bit. When you start writing your own programs any errors in the *syntax*, i.e. the rules of the Python language, will result in an error message being scrolled across the grid of LEDs. There are no errors in **'Hello, World!'** so it should run automatically.

Tap the **Download** button on the editor shown on the right and on the previous page. This translates the program to a *hexadecimal file (.hex)* as discussed in more detail in Appendix 1. The following menu bar is displayed:

Save

The **Save** button shown above automatically stores a copy of the program as a *.hex file* in the **Downloads** folder of your computer, as shown below in the Windows 10 File Explorer.

Save as

The **Save as** button as shown on the right of the menu bar on the previous page lets you give the file a name and save it in a folder of your choice in the file manager of your computer, such as the File Explorer in Windows 10.

In this example I called the file **hello.hex** and saved it in a new folder called **my HEX files** on the C: drive i.e. hard disc drive.

Now connect the micro:bit to the computer using a USB cable. The micro:bit should show up in the file manager just like any other external device such as the flash drive **KINGSTON (H:)** shown below.

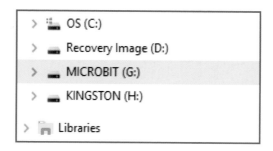

Now drag and drop the .hex file onto the micro:bit name listed as **MICROBIT (G:)** in the file manager, as shown below in the Windows 10 File Explorer.

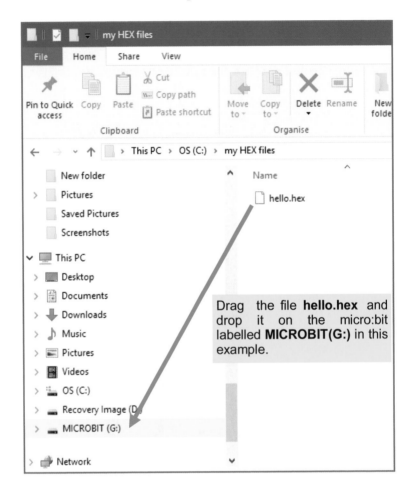

Drag the file **hello.hex** and drop it on the micro:bit labelled **MICROBIT(G:)** in this example.

The Status LED on the back of the micro:bit (shown on page 4) starts flashing while the .hex file is copied from the computer to the micro:bit.

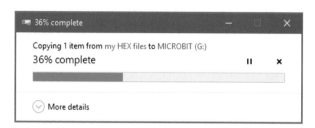

The Status LED stops flashing when the program has been completely copied to the micro:bit. The program is then run or executed automatically.

In this example the message 'Hello, World!' is scrolled from left to right across the grid of 5 x 5 LEDs. This is achieved by the statement shown below and on page 13.

```
6    display.scroll('Hello, World!')
```

Next Line 7 is executed, displaying an image of a heart in red on the grid of LEDs, as shown below.

```
7    display.show(Image.HEART)
```

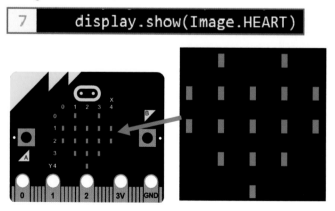

The Browser Editor Buttons

This chapter showed how to start using the browser editor by copying a pre-written program and running it on the micro:bit. Chapter 4 is intended to help you start entering and running your own programs. Listed below are the tools provided in the browser editor and shown in the screenshot on page 13.

 Download the source code from the editor in the browser, so that it can be saved as a **.hex** file on your computer. Discussed in detail on page 14.

 Save your code on your computer in the standard Python **.py** file format. Save in the **Downloads** folder or a location of your choice.

 Snippets are abbreviations, shown on the next page, which represent pieces of MicroPython code. They can easily be inserted in your program to save typing the code.

 Help. This displays several pages of help and documentation including sample programs and cartoons by Mike Rowbit.

 **Zoom-in i.e.** enlarge the text.

Zoom-out.

Snippets

When you select the **Snippets** icon shown on the previous page and on page 13, the list of snippets shown in part below appears. The triggers are abbreviations for common MicroPython pieces of code for different tasks.

⚙ Code Snippets

Code snippets are short blocks of code to re-use in your own programs. There are snippets fo common things you'll want to do using MicroPython.

Select one of the snippets below, or type the snippet's *trigger* then tap the TAB key.

trigger	description
docs	create a comment to describe your code
wh	while some condition is True, keep looping over some code
with	do stuff with something assigned to a name
cl	create a new class that defines the behaviour of a new type of object
def	define a named function that takes some arguments and optionally add a des

If you click on a snippet description such as **while some condition is True** above, or type the trigger **wh** and press the Tab key, the piece of code is inserted into the editor ready for you to complete the line, as shown below

```
10 ▾ while condition:
11        # TODO: write code...
```

In this example we might add a *condition* such as counter < 20 to complete line 10, which then becomes:

```
10   while counter < 20:
```

This means "while the number in the store called counter is less than 20 keep repeating the indented block of lines below this one."

MicroPython *reserved words* or *keywords* such as while are discussed in Chapter 4.

Summary

- Programs can be written in the MicroPython browser editor at the Web site *microbit.org*.

- *Snippets* allow pieces of code to be entered by selecting from a list or typing a *trigger* or abbreviation, instead of typing all of the words.

- The program is *downloaded* from the Internet and saved on the laptop or desktop computer as a *hexadecimal* (*.hex*) file, using a *file manager* program such as Windows 10 File Explorer.

- The micro:bit is then connected to the computer using a *USB cable*.

- The file is *dragged* in the file manager and *dropped* onto the micro:bit, which is listed as a removable device, like a flash drive. This *copies* the .hex code to the micro:bit and the program *runs automatically* when the copying is complete.

- The *status light* on the back of the micro:bit flashes while the program is being copied.

- The program stays in the *flash memory* of the micro:bit until it's overwritten by a new program.

- The *program reset button* on the back of the micro:bit can be used to restart and run a program currently in the memory.

- The browser editor is easy to launch and use but copying a program to the micro:bit is more complicated than using the *Flash* button in the Mu editor discussed in Chapter 3.

Introducing the Mu Editor

Introduction

Like the Web browser editor discussed in Chapter 2, Mu is a source code editor written in the Python language. Both editors were written by Nicholas Tollervey and are designed to be easy for beginners to use.

Unlike the Web browser editor, Mu is stored *locally* on your computer's hard disc drive, not on the Internet.

So Mu has to be installed on your computer. However, this is a one-off task and once Mu is installed you can start creating and editing programs, even if you haven't got an Internet connection. As discussed shortly, a simple click of the *Flash* button in Mu is all you need to copy a program you've written in Mu and run it on the micro:bit. This is simpler than the browser editor's method of downloading your program then dragging and dropping it to the micro:bit in a file manager, as described in Chapter 2.

Mu is downloaded from the following Web site:

https://codewith.mu

Code With Mu

Mu is a simple code editor for beginner programmers. It's written in Python and works on Windows, OSX, Linux and Raspberry Pi.

Download now   Help

On selecting the **Download now** button shown at the bottom of the previous page, you can select which version of Mu to download, depending on your computer's operating system — Windows, OSX or Linux.

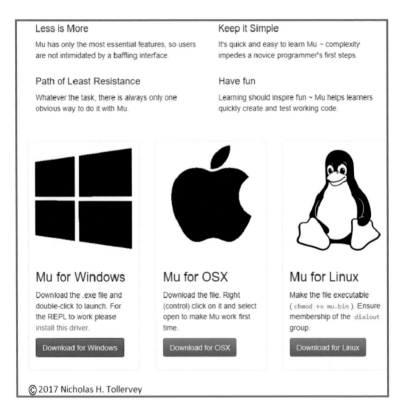

Less is More

Mu has only the most essential features, so users are not intimidated by a baffling interface.

Keep it Simple

It's quick and easy to learn Mu ~ complexity impedes a novice programmer's first steps.

Path of Least Resistance

Whatever the task, there is always only one obvious way to do it with Mu.

Have fun

Learning should inspire fun ~ Mu helps learners quickly create and test working code.

Mu for Windows

Download the .exe file and double-click to launch. For the REPL to work please install this driver.

Download for Windows

Mu for OSX

Download the file. Right (control) click on it and select open to make Mu work first time.

Download for OSX

Mu for Linux

Make the file executable (chmod +x mu.bin). Ensure membership of the dialout group.

Download for Linux

© 2017 Nicholas H. Tollervey

If you select **Download for Windows** shown above there is a link "**install this driver**" to enable a piece of Mu software called *REPL* (Read, Evaluate, Print and Loop) to work on your computer. This lets you type in single MicroPython commands and quickly test them to make sure the *syntax* or grammar is correct. REPL is discussed in Chapter 5.

Installing the Mu Editor

Select the appropriate blue download button shown on the previous page. You are given options to save the file as shown below.

What do you want to do with mu-0.9.13.win.exe (27.7 MB)?
From: github-cloud.s3.amazonaws.com

Save Save as

Save above places a copy of the Mu **.exe** file in the **Download** folder on your computer. (An **.exe** file or *application* is used to run or *execute* a program).

Save as above places a copy of the Mu .exe file in a folder of your choice such as **My Mu folder** shown below.

mu .exe file

> This PC > OS (C:) > My Mu folder

OneDrive

This PC

Name

mu-0.9.13.win.exe

Installing Mu is a one-off task and you can now run it by double-clicking it's name in your file manager such as the Windows File Explorer. Alternatively, in Windows, right-click the Mu **.exe** file as shown in blue above and select **Send to > Desktop (create shortcut)**, shown below to create a Mu icon as shown on the right.

Send to	>	🔵 Bluetooth device
Cut		🔲 Compressed (zipped) folder
Copy		⬛ Desktop (create shortcut)

Getting Started with Mu

Launching Mu

The Mu editor can be launched by double-clicking its name in its folder in your file manager or its icon on the desktop, as shown on the previous page.

The Mu editor screen opens as shown below, ready for you to start entering your first program:

1 from microbit import * , already inserted above, makes sure all the ready-made pieces of MicroPython code, such as images, are ready for you to use, as discussed later.

Lines beginning with # as in # Write your code here :-) are *comments* or helpful notes, not commands to be executed in the micro:bit.

As can be seen above, there are more icons or buttons in Mu representing different tasks than in the browser editor discussed in Chapter 2, page 18. However, the Mu editor, like the browser editor, also created by Nicholas Tollervey, is still very easy to use and makes the copying of your scripts to the micro:bit a very simple task.

Mu Buttons

The buttons shown on page 24 have the following functions:

Opens a blank page in Mu to start a new *script* i.e. a program or piece of source code, as shown on page 24. It will initially have the name **untitled**.

Retrieves a file that you saved previously so that you can edit the script and run the program.

Saves the file on your computer's hard drive in the **.py** Python file format. You can create a new folder for your files and make up a file name, such as **counter.py** in a folder such as **Mu code**. In Windows, the path to the file would then be:

This PC > OS(C:) > Mu code > counter.py

Copies or *flash*es your code to the memory of the micro:bit and runs it straightaway.

Displays a list of the Mu files you've created.

This button allows you to enter single lines of code to quickly check that they are correct.

REPL stands for *Read Eval Print Loop*.

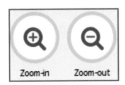

Makes the code listed on the screen bigger or smaller.

Changes the background on the Mu screen from white to black or vice versa.

Checks your code and underlines any errors.

Lists the functions of the Mu buttons.

Ends the current session with Mu. You are prompted to save your work, if necessary.

Programming in the Mu Editor

Mu doesn't open with a sample program already entered, unlike the browser editor shown on page 13. Shown below is a program for you to enter in Exercise 1 on page 28. It's similar to the program on page 13. The program is explained in detail in Chapter 4.

You will need a computer with the Mu editor installed as described earlier. Also a USB cable for connecting the micro:bit to the computer

```
1    from microbit import *
2
3    # Write your code here   :-)
4
5    counter = 1
6
7    while counter < 11:
8        display.scroll("Hi, Everyone!")
9        display.show(Image.BUTTERFLY)
10       counter = counter+1
11       sleep(10000)
```

Some notes intended to help you enter the program avoiding common errors are given on the next page.

(You could also enter and run this program using the Web browser editor discussed in Chapter 2, if you haven't yet installed Mu on your computer).

Exercise 1: Entering the Code

- Copy the code on page 27 <u>exactly</u> into your computer. Line 3 is a *comment* and can be omitted.

- Blank lines can be entered by pressing the **Enter** or **Return** key. This can make programs easier to read.

- Use lower case (small) letters except where capital letters are shown.

- Make sure the *colon* (:) is entered at the end of line 7. This automatically indents lines 8-11 by 4 spaces.

- Brackets (also known as *parentheses*) must be inserted in pairs, as in:

  Sleep(10000)

- Full stops (.) must be inserted after keywords such as display and Image, as shown below:

  display.scroll   Image.BUTTERFLY

- Inverted commas, also known as quotes or speech marks, should be inserted in pairs. Both double and single quotes are allowed (in pairs), as shown below.

  ('Hi, Everyone!')   ("Hi, Everyone!")

- Select the **Check** button shown on the right and on pages 24 and 26. Any mistakes in your code, known as *syntax errors* will be underlined.

- Finally select the **Save** button and save the program as **.py** file with a name such as **counter.py** in a folder of your choice.

Copying the Code to the micro:bit

After entering all of the code:

- Connect the micro:bit to your computer using a USB cable, as shown on page 5.

- Select the **Flash** button, shown on the right and on pages 24 and 25.

- The Status LED on the back of the micro:bit flashes while the code is copied and saved on the micro:bit.

Flash

- The Status LED stops flashing and the program is then run or executed on the micro:bit.

So with a single click, Mu has detected and located the attached micro:bit, created a new *.hex* file from your program and copied this file over to the micro:bit. Mu uses a Python utility program called *uFlash*, pronounced "micro flash", to carry out the flashing process. All being well you should see the message "**Hi, Everyone!**" scrolled across the LEDs followed by the **BUTTERFLY** image, as shown below.

If you make an error in your code, the LEDs display a message such as **Line 7 Syntax Error**.

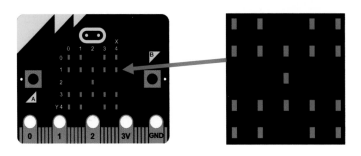

Summary

- The Mu editor is a program written in Python and installed on your computer hard disc drive, etc.

- You can launch Mu by double-clicking its .exe file in its location in your file manager. Or create a *shortcut icon* on the desktop to launch Mu by double- clicking.

- Programs can be written and edited in the MicroPython Mu editor.

- Mu allows you to save and retrieve your programs as files in the standard *.py Python file format*.

- Mu has a **Check** button which underlines *syntax errors* in your scripts or source code.

- When typing a script or source code, it's essential to obey the syntax or rules of the Micropython language, with regard to brackets, speech marks, colons, spacing and indentation, etc..

- Mu works with an *REPL* program (Read, Evaluate, Print and Loop) which allows you to type in a single line of code and test it immediately.

- A single click of the Mu **Flash** button copies your program code from the Mu editor, translates it into a .hex file and quickly runs it on the BBC micro:bit.

Starting to Program

Introduction

This chapter is intended to help you understand the program shown below and on page 27.

```
1   from microbit import *
2
3   # Write your code here   :-)
4
5   counter = 1
6
7   while counter < 11:
8       display.scroll("Hi, Everyone!")
9       display.show(Image.BUTTERFLY)
10      counter = counter+1
11      sleep(10000)
```

- Words shown in blue above are *keywords* built into the MicroPython language.

- Words and numbers shown in red are specified by the programmer and are not built into MicroPython.

- Lines starting with #, such as line 3 shown in black above, are *comments*, for information only.

The Program in Detail

The following *statements* or lines of code are shown on the program listing on the previous page.

```
1  from microbit  import  *
```

Programming languages such as Python and MicroPython have ready-made, frequently-used pieces of coding which you can *import* into your program to save coding it yourself everytime it's needed. The asterisk (*) means *everything in the MicroPython library*. So this line means "make available to my program all of the pre-written coding such as images, i.e. pictures, etc." The library also contains *modules* such as the math module containing *functions* like square roots.

```
2
```

Blank lines such as lines 2, 4 and 6 can be inserted to make a program easier to read.

```
3   # Write your code here  :-)
```

Statements starting with (#) are simply *comments* i.e. notes intended to help people understand a program. They are not executed like the program commands.

```
5 counter = 1
```

This creates a *store* in the computer's memory and assigns the value 1 to it. You make up your own name, such as counter, but these should not be MicroPython keywords.

7   while counter <11:

This means "while the *condition* which follows is True, keep repeating the block of *indented* lines below". In this case the condition is that the number in the store called counter is less than (<) 11. This is an example of a while loop and is discussed again in more detail on page 34.

8   display.scroll("Hi, Everyone!")

Scroll the message **"Hi, Everyone!"** from right to left across the matrix of 5 x 5 LEDs on the micro:bit .

9   display.show(Image.BUTTERFLY)

Display the MicroPython image of the **BUTTERFLY** on the LEDs on the micro:bit, as shown on page 29.

10   counter = counter+1

This adds 1 to the number in store counter each time the loop is executed.

11   sleep(10000)

This causes the program to pause for 10000 milliseconds, i.e. 10 seconds, before looping back up to line 7.

The while **Loop in More Detail**

```
7   while counter < 11:

8       display.scroll("Hi, Everyone!")

9       display.show(Image.BUTTERFLY)

10      counter = counter + 1

11      sleep(10000)
```

- counter was initially set at 1 in line 5 of the program.
- while the condition at line 7 is True, i.e. the number in store counter is less than 11, lines 8-11 are repeatedly executed in a series of passes or loops.
- With each pass down lines 8-11 the number in counter is increased by 1, i.e. counter successively contains 1, 2, 3, 4.....11.
- When counter reaches 11, i.e. not less than 11, the condition at line 7 is no longer true and the loop ends.
- The program will continue downwards to execute commands below the end of the loop if there are any.

The output from this program is the message "**Hi, Everyone!**" scrolled across the LEDs followed by the image of a butterfly on the LEDs, as shown on page 29. After pausing for 10 seconds this is repeated a further 9 times.

An Infinite Loop

If we change line 7 to that shown on the right, this condition will always be

```
7   while True:
```

True, (since True is always True) so the loop and the displays on the LEDs will continue indefinitely or until you disconnect the micro:bit from the computer.

Variable Names

These are names that you use to label the store locations in the computer's memory containing pieces of data. For example, counter was used in the program on page 31 to temporarily hold a number as it changed or *varied* from 1 to 11 with each pass through the loop.

You can make up your own variable names. In the previous example you might have used number instead of counter, for example.

Numeric Variables

Numeric variables contain mathematical numbers, i.e. numbers which can used in calculations, such as:

> number_in_stock=19

Variable names should, if possible, be meaningful, to help other people understand your program. The underscore (_) can be added to improve readability.

String Variables

Strings can contain letters and punctuation marks, as in "**Hi, Everyone!**".

Strings are enclosed in speech marks. They can also include non-mathematical numbers, as in:

> post_code="SE476NR"

Here, 476 is just three separate *characters* rather than the number four hundred and seventy six. Other strings using numbers as characters include telephone numbers, account numbers, car registrations and PIN numbers.

Exercise 2: Editing a Program in Mu

This exercise modifies the program shown on page 27.

The same program was used in Exercise 1. If you successfully completed Exercise 1 you should be able to retrieve it by using the Mu **LOAD** button, shown on pages 24 and 25.

Alternatively copy the program exactly as it is on page 27, but without line 3, which is not necessary now.

- Change the variable name counter to a name of your choice, wherever it occurs throughout the program .

- Change the while condition so that the message and Image are displayed 5 times not 10 as before.

- Change the message to scroll several words of your own, instead of ("Hi, Everyone!").

- Change the Image to one of the others in the MicroPython library, such as:

  Image.HAPPY   Image.SAD   Image.RABBIT

- Change line 11 so that the program only pauses for 5 seconds, not 10 as previously.

- Click the **Check** button and if necessary correct any underlined errors.

- Connect a USB cable and click the **Flash** button to run the program on the micro:bit.

- The program should run and scroll your message on the LEDs. After a pause of 5 seconds the message and the Image should be repeated 4 more times.

If there are any errors in the program you'll see a scrolled error message such as **Line 9 Syntax Error**.

Computer code must be exactly right and what might seem a trivial mistake can cause the program to fail. As discussed on page 28 common errors include:

- MicroPython reserved words spelt incorrectly, e.g. desplay instead of display.

- Missing colon (:) at line 7 and therefore no indentation on lines 8-11.

- Missing speech marks as in:

  display.scroll(Hi, Everyone!")

- Missing bracket, as in sleep10000).

- No full stop, as in displayshow.

If you've made any errors, correct them in the Mu editor then click to **Flash** and run the program.

When the program is correct click the **Save** button, give the file a name and save it as a **.py** file in a folder of your choice, so that it's available to **LOAD** in future, if necessary.

You might also like to change line 7 to while True: to check out the infinite loop, as discussed at the bottom of page 34.

The while Loop

Loops allow a computer to repeat a block of code a specified number of times. So it's just as easy to repeat a process 1000 times as it is to repeat it five times, for example. Simply alter the condition after while as follows:

while number < 6:   while number < 1001:

Summary

- The import command allows your program to use the *library* of pre-written *modules* in MicroPython.

- Lines starting with # are *comments* to explain parts of a program and are not executable code.

- The while loop repeats the *indented* block of code which follows the while statement as long as the specified *condition* is True.

- If the condition is always True the loop continues indefinitely until the micro:bit is unplugged.

- *Variable names* are labels assigned by the user to *stores* (like tiny boxes) in the computer's memory.

- *Numeric variables* contain only mathematical numbers, i.e. those which can be used in counting and calculations, etc., such as the following:

  $$age = 27 \qquad speed = 75$$

- *String variables* are used to store data consisting of letters, names, etc., or a mixture of letters, numbers and punctuation marks. The data in a string is enclosed in speech marks, as shown below.

  $$name = \text{"Stella"} \qquad reg\_no = \text{"PY16MIC"}$$

- If you make an error in the *data* in a string, such as someones's name, this won't stop the program running. Unlike *syntax errors*, such as the incorrect use of brackets, punctuation marks, speech marks and the mis-spelling of MicroPython *keywords*.

5

REPL: Interactive Coding

Introduction

REPL stands for *Read-Eval-Print-Loop*. It's a feature within MicroPython and other programming languages. As shown on pages 24 and 26 and below, there is a button to launch REPL from within the Mu editor.

When you select the REPL button shown on the right and below, REPL opens with a prompt in the lower half of the screen, below the normal Mu editor window.

Repl

```
from microbit import *

# Write your code here :-)

counter = 1

while counter < 11:
    display.scroll('Hi, Everyone!')
    display.show(Image.BUTTERFLY)
    counter = counter+1
    sleep(10000)
```
>>> **REPL prompt**

```
>>>
```

After you type a line of code at the prompt and press **Enter** or **Return**, the line is immediately interpreted, i.e. translated, and then executed.

So REPL is a very quick way to test and experiment with single lines of code or small groups of lines, to make sure they work and that the *syntax*, i.e. grammar, is correct.

Setting up REPL

It was stated on page 22 that Windows users should **"install this driver"**, a piece of software to enable the REPL to work. Although I was able to use REPL in Windows 10 without installing the driver software, it is needed by earlier versions of Windows such as Windows XP and Windows Vista.

Repl

To download the driver, in your Web browser enter **https://codewith.mu** and from the resulting Web page select **"install this driver"**, as shown below and on page 22.

Then follow the instructions on the screen, as shown below, to download and install the driver software. The micro:bit (known here as **mbed**) must be connected to your computer during the installation process, step 2 shown below.

1. Download the mbed Windows serial port driver

Download the installer to your PC, e.g. your desktop.

Download latest driver

2. Run the installer

With your **mbed plugged in**, and *no explorer drive windows open*, run the installer:

Using REPL

Connect the micro:bit to the computer using a USB cable.

Open Mu as described on pages 24 then select the REPL button shown on page 40. REPL opens in a new window in the lower half of the screen, displaying the prompt shown on the right. (Don't type it).

> > >

Enter the following line and press **Enter** or **Return**.

```
>>>   from microbit import *
>>>
```

Now enter a line you want to test, such as the line below starting with display and then press **Enter** or **Return**.

```
>>>   from microbit import *
>>>   display.scroll("Hi, Everyone!")
>>>
```

If the display line above is correct **"Hi, Everyone!"** is immediately scrolled across the LEDs on the micro:bit and then a new prompt (> > >) is displayed as shown above.

If you make a mistake in the code, an error message appears, as shown below:

Error

```
>>>   display.show(image.DUCK)

Traceback "<stdin>", line 1, in <module>
NameError: name 'image' is not defined
>>>
```

Error message

This time REPL has found a mistake and displayed the error message shown on the previous page. In MicroPython only "Image" is used to display graphics i.e. pictures. The error message on page 39 says "image" is not defined.

The correct version of the display statement is shown below.

```
>>>   display.show(Image.DUCK)
>>>
```

On pressing **Enter** or **Return**, the image of a duck appears *immediately* on the LEDs on the attached micro:bit.

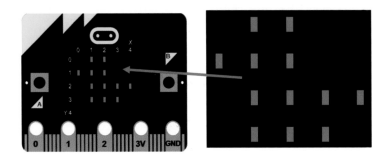

A new prompt appears as shown on the right, ready for you to enter and test another line of code.

Auto-Complete

When typing in commands in REPL mode and in Mu in general, this feature can save a lot of time. Just type the first two or three letters then press the Tab key. For example, type di then press the Tab key to fully enter "display", a MicroPython keyword.

Getting Help

Enter help() after the prompt in REPL and press **Enter** or **Return** to get some hints and tips and useful commands.

To get help about a particular MicroPython word, such as the sleep command, type help(sleep) and press **Enter** or **Return**. The following appears:

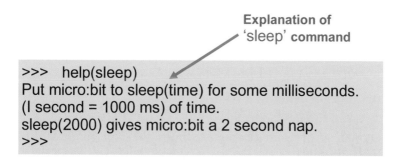

Explanation of 'sleep' command

```
>>>  help(sleep)
Put micro:bit to sleep(time) for some milliseconds.
(I second = 1000 ms) of time.
sleep(2000) gives micro:bit a 2 second nap.
>>>
```

You might also try entering each of the following as single commands on a separate line, pressing **Enter** or **Return** after each one. A new prompt should appear automatically, at the end of the help notes, as shown above.

Scroll up and down to see all of your REPL commands.

```
>>>  help(display.scroll)
```
```
>>>  help(compass)
```

```
>>>  help(display.show)
```
```
>>>  help(Image)
```

```
>>>  help(temperature)
```
```
>>>  help(panic)
```

```
>>>  help(accelerometer)
```
```
>>>  help(button_a)
```

Further Help

If you typed the help commands at the bottom of the previous page the responses on the screen should have helped you understand the various MicroPython keywords. However, if you have not yet started using MicroPython, the help notes are briefly summarised below.

display.scroll

Scrolls a *string*, i.e. a group of letters, characters, etc., as discussed on page 38, across the array of 5 x 5 LEDs on the micro:bit.

Including a delay in a scrolled message

To *scroll* the message "Have a nice day!" with a *delay* of 2 seconds after each character, enter the following at the REPL prompt:

>>> display.scroll("Have a nice day!", 2000)

Please note the full stop, brackets, speech marks and comma.

display.show

Display a single image on the micro:bit such as the duck shown on page 42.

Showing a string one character at a time

To *show* a string of characters one character at a time with a *delay* of 3 seconds, enter the following at the REPL prompt:

>>> display.show("Have a nice day!", 3000)

temperature

Displays the temperature of the micro:bit in degrees Celsius, as shown below.

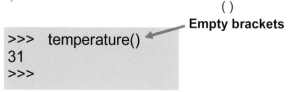

( )
Empty brackets

```
>>>   temperature()
31
>>>
```

accelerometer

Detects the micro-bit's movement in 3 dimensions as discussed later in this book.

compass

Uses the earth's magnetic fields to detect the direction the micro:bit is moving in.

Image

Use built-in images such as Image.RABBIT or design your own images by programming the 5 x 5 LED grid on the micro:bit as discussed in Chapter 6.

panic

This puts the micro:bit into a panic mode and displays an unhappy face.

```
>>>   panic()
```

To exit panic mode, press the program reset button on the back of the micro:bit, as shown on page 4.

button_a

Button **A** on the micro:bit. Used with is_pressed() to execute certain statements when pressed down, as discussed on page 96. Button **B** is programmed in a similar way.

Exercise 3: Using REPL to Check Code

Make sure you have a micro:bit connected to your computer by USB cable. The following 3 commands all include one or more deliberate errors.

>>> from micobit import *

>>> display.scroll(Punctuation really matters"

>>> displayshow(Image.heart)

See if you can spot the errors and type the correct version at the REPL prompt. After pressing **Enter** or **Return**, if your line is correct any output should appear on the 5 x 5 LEDs and you should see the 3-arrows prompt as shown below.

>>> display.show(Image.GIRAFFE)
>>>

If you can't see the errors in the top 3 commands on this page, type the lines in exactly as shown and try to use any resulting error messages to find the mistake and type the correct command. For example, if you spell GIRAFFE wrongly as GIRAFE you would get the error message shown below.

'MicroBit Image' has no attribute 'GIRAFE'

(This means there is no GIRAFE image in the MicroPython library, only a GIRAFFE.)

The correct versions of the 3 lines at the top of this page containing deliberate mistakes are shown on page 48.

Using REPL to test several lines of code
Enter the code shown below at the REPL prompt.

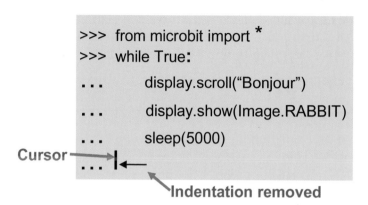

```
>>>  from microbit import *
>>>  while True:
...          display.scroll("Bonjour")
...          display.show(Image.RABBIT)
...          sleep(5000)
...  |←—
```

Cursor

Indentation removed

After entering the colon(:) in while True: and pressing **Enter** or **Return**:

- The prompt changes to three dots (…) .
- Each line is indented by 4 spaces.
- After entering sleep(5000) the flashing cursor appears indented 4 spaces.
- Press the *backspace key* to remove the indentation.
- Press **Enter** or **Return** to execute all of the lines of code.
- In this example the word "Bonjour" is scrolled across the 5 x 5 LEDs followed by the image of a rabbit.
- The program pauses for 5 seconds.
- While True: is always true, so the while loop is repeated indefinitely until you press **CTRL_C** or disconnect the micro:bit.

CTRL_C: Hold down the **CTRL** key and press **C** to stop a program currently running.

Summary

- *REPL* is an *interactive mode* within the Mu editor which allows you to run or *execute* statements one at a time as soon you press **Enter** or **Return**. So you can experiment to find the correct syntax.

- The micro:bit must be connected to your computer to launch REPL using its button. The REPL `>>>` *prompt* should appear automatically.

- If a command is correct, any *output* such as a message or an image will appear on the 5 x 5 LEDs and the REPL prompt will appear on the next line.

- If a line contains a mistake, an *error message* identifying the error is displayed on the screen.

- You can enter several lines such as a while loop. Lines after the colon have a *3-dot prompt* and are indented by 4 spaces. To execute the code use the backspace key to remove the indentation on the line after the last statement, then press **Enter** or **Return**.

- To save typing time, just enter the first 3 letters of MicroPython keywords, then press the Tab key to *auto-complete* the keyword.

- Press **CTRL_C** to stop a program currently running in REPL, such as an infinite loop.

The correct lines in Exercise 3, page 46 are:

```
>>> from microbit import *
```

```
>>> display.scroll("Punctuation really matters")
```

```
>>> display.show(Image.heart)
```

Viewing and Creating Images in MicroPython

Introduction

Earlier chapters have shown that a large number of ready-made images are available in MicroPython. These can be built into your programs and displayed on the grid of 5 x 5 LEDs on the front of the BBC micro:bit, as shown in the three samples below.

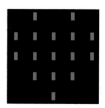 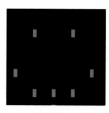 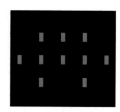

Image.HEART   Image.SMILE   Image.TORTOISE

This chapter shows how you can:

- Use a Website to view on your computer screen an accurate simulation of the BBC micro:bit. This includes, amongst other useful features, displaying all the available images in the MicroPython library. Also scrolling messages across the array of 5 x 5 LEDs.

- Design and test your own images in REPL mode and build them into your own programs in the Mu editor.

- Also *saving* programs created in Mu in the **.py** file format so they can be *loaded* or retrieved at a later time.

Using a micro:bit Simulator on the Web

This is a Website created by Nicholas Tollervey. It allows you to replicate on your computer screen some of the main functions of the micro:bit. These include the output from the micro:bit such as the display of images. Also the scrolling of messages on the matrix of 5 x 5 LEDs.

Enter the following address into a Web browser such as Microsoft Edge, Internet Explorer, Google Chrome or Apple Safari:

http://pycomic.github.io/microbit.html

The Web page opens as shown below:

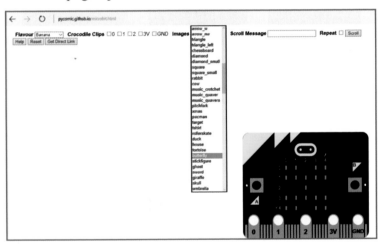

The options for displaying images and scrolling messages appear on the top right-hand side of the screen, as shown at the top of the next page.

The above simulator is a very good resource for learning about the micro:bit. Also for producing screenshots for use in reports, documentation and educational material.

Viewing Images

Select the down arrow to the right of **Images** shown above to display a drop-down menu of the available images. An extract from the menu is shown below and can be scrolled to see the full list of images. Select the image you want such as **butterfly** and this appears on the micro:bit as shown on the next page and on page 50.

Scrolling a Message

Enter the text in the **Scroll Message** bar shown at top of this page, then select the **Scroll** button at the top right. To scroll a message continuously in the **Scroll Message** bar, tick the **Repeat** box first, then select **Scroll**.

Shown below is the left-hand side of the BBC micro:bit as viewed on the Website, also shown on page 50.

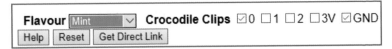

The micro:bit is available in various colour schemes, which can be selected from the drop-down menu next to **Flavour**, shown above. The micro:bit below is shown in the **Mint** colour scheme, while the device on page 50 is in **Banana**.

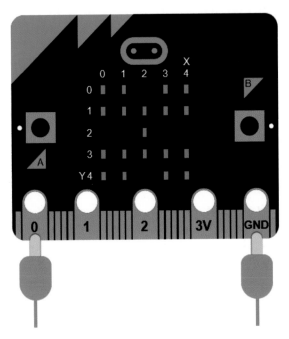

Crocodile Clips in the menu bar at the top of the page and shown diagrammatically in red above, illustrate how the BBC micro:bit can be connected to various external devices such as speakers and robots.

Creating Your Own Images

This section shows how to design an image and include it in a MicroPython program to be displayed as output on the micro:bit LEDs.

To display an image of a dog, for example, you might want to do a quick sketch on paper as shown on the left below, to get an idea of how the dog will look on the 5 x 5 matrix of LEDs on the front of the BBC micro:bit.

LEDs which are switched on with maximum brightness are coded with a 9 while 0 is used for LEDs which are off. Numbers between 0 and 9 can be used to give varying levels of brightness on the LEDs. So the dog might be coded as shown on the right below.

```
0 9 0 0 0
9 9 0 0 0
9 9 9 9 9
0 9 9 9 9
0 9 0 0 9
```

Sketch on paper   **Coding for the dog**

The dog could be coded as:

```
dog=Image("09000:"
          "99000:"
          "99999:"
          "09999:"
          "09009")
```

Alternatively, the image of the dog could be coded in a single line, starting with the top row of the LED grid shown on the previous page and working downwards, as follows:

Note the use of the brackets, speech marks and the colon. The colon (:) is not needed after 09009 above, which represents the bottom row of LEDs shown on page 53.

Exercise 4: Creating Your Own Image

- Think of a simple image that you would like to code. A few ideas are shown below.

- If necessary to visualise your image, sketch out the 5 x 5 matrix of LEDs on paper and colour or shade those needed to be switched on to display the image.

- Write out the matrix of LEDs using 0's and 9's similar to that shown on page 53.

- Choose a suitable name for your image and write out the coding using the 5 x 5 matrix similar to the coding for the dog at the bottom of page 53.

- Write your image as a single line of your own code, as shown above and replacing dog with the name you've chosen for your image. This code will be needed shortly.

Exercise 5: Testing in REPL Mode

Your new image can be tested quickly in the REPL mode in Mu, as discussed in Chapter 5.

- Connect the micro:bit to your computer.
- Select the **Repl** button shown on the right.
- A new 3-arrow prompt should appear in the REPL panel in the bottom half of the Mu screen as shown below.

- Enter the ever present "import all" line shown below, then press **Enter** or **Return**:

>>> from microbit import *

- Enter your single line of coding for your own image, similar to the line shown below, followed by **Enter** or **Return**.

>>>dog=Image("09000:99000:99999:09999:09009")

- Enter the display.show command as shown below, but including the name of your own image. Then press **Enter** or **Return**.

>>> display.show(dog)

- Your new image should appear instantly on the matrix of 5 x 5 LEDs, as shown below for the dog.

Coding an Image Using Separate Rows

Alternatively, you may prefer to enter the image in 5 separate rows as it appears on the 5 x 5 matrix of LEDs, as shown below. After typing the first two lines and pressing **Enter** or **Return**, a 3-dot prompt appears until all 5 rows of the LEDs have been entered. Then the 3-arrow prompt returns, allowing you to enter the display.show command, shown below, to light up the image on the micro:bit.

```
>>> from microbit import *
>>> dog=Image("09000:"
... "99000:"
... "99999:"
... "09999:"
... "09009")
>>> display.show(dog)
>>>
```

You may prefer to line up the rows of 0's and 9's underneath one another using the space bar, as shown below. This doesn't affect the validity of the lines of coding either in the REPL interactive mode or in programs coded and saved in the Mu editor.

```
>>> from microbit import *
>>> dog=Image("09000:"
...            "99000:"
...            "99999:"
...            "09999:"
...            "09009")
>>> display.show(dog)
>>>
```

Exercise 6: Programming Your Image

This exercise requires you to enter the program below, but modified to display your own scrolled text message and your own image.

```
1   from microbit  import *
2
3   dog= Image("09000:99000:99999:09999:09099")
4
5   counter = 1
6   while counter < 6:
7           display.scroll("Say hello to Lassie")
8           display.show(dog)
9           counter = counter+1
10          sleep(5000)
```

- Select **New** from the Mu menu bar.
- Make sure Line 1 is entered.
- Enter your own variable name instead of dog and your own Image as a single line 3.
- Change line 6 to display the output 10 times.
- Type your own message on line 7.
- Change line 10 to pause the program for 10 seconds.
- Select the **Save** button to make a copy of the program in a folder of your choice on your computer, as discussed on pages 58 and 59.
- Select **Flash** to copy the program to the micro:bit and display the message and image on the LEDs.
- Repeat the program coding the image in 5 rows as shown on page 56.

Saving and Loading Programs

When you **Flash** a program to the micro:bit it is not readily available to retrieve back to your computer for editing or developing at a later date. So you need to make copies of programs on your computer's *internal storage* — usually a *hard disc drive* or an *SSD (Solid State Drive)*. Or perhaps a removable *flash drive/memory stick* if you want to transfer your MicroPython (.py) files between computers.

When developing larger programs over a period of time, it's essential that you keep saving the latest version — otherwise you'll have to keep retyping the code.

When you select **New** from the Mu menu bar, as shown below, a blank screen appears ready for you to type in a new program. The default file name **untitled** appears at the top left of the screen, as shown below.

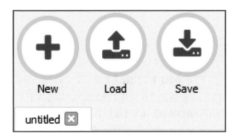

After entering the program select the **Save** button shown above. As it's a new program you are given the chance to select a folder on your computer and enter a **File name**.

File name:	
Save as type:	
	Save

In this example I had already created (in Windows 10 File Explorer), a **Mu Code** folder within a folder called **Microbit** in my **OneDrive** as shown below. The **.py** (*Python file type*) extension is added automatically as shown below — you can't enter a file type in **Save as type** shown on the previous page.

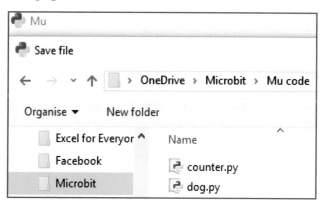

Retrieving a Saved Program (.py) File

When you want to recover a file you've previously saved, select **Load** on the Mu menu bar, as shown on the previous page. This opens your file manager, such as File Explorer where you can browse to the folder containing your .py files, as shown above during the **Save** operation.

Select the file you want to retrieve such as **dog.py** and select the **Open** button shown below.

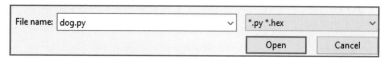

The retrieved program file should now be displayed in Mu, with its name on the menu bar across the top of the screen.

Summary

- The following Website allows you to simulate and visualize many of the functions of the BBC micro:bit and easily make useful screenshots.

  http://pycomic.github.io/microbit.html

- You can create your *own images* by coding a 5 x 5 grid representing the LEDs on the micro:bit. 9 and 0 are used to represent LEDs switched On and Off respectively. Numbers 1 to 9 can be used for varying levels of brightness.

- Your image can be coded in the following format:

  ```
  dog=Image("09000:99000:99999:09999:09009")
  ```

  Each group of 5 digits, working from left to right above, represents a row of the 5 x 5 matrix of LEDs, working from top to bottom of the matrix.

- Your newly created image can be tested in the *interactive REPL mode*, before including it in a full size program in the Mu editor.

- Programs are saved in the Mu editor using the **Save** button at the top of the screen. Files are saved in the normal Python *.py file format*.

- The first time you save a file, you are able to select a *folder* for the program using your computer's file manager, such as Windows File Explorer.

- Programs can be retrieved later, for editing and developing in the Mu editor, after selecting the Mu **Load** button and browsing to the relevant folder.

Animation in MicroPython

Introduction

The last chapter showed how you can:

- Use a Website to view the vast library of ready-made images in MicroPython and simulate some of the other activities possible with the BBC micro:bit.

- Also create and code your own images by lighting up the relevant LEDs on the 5x5 matrix on the micro:bit.

This chapter shows how to take an image you've created and move it across the LED matrix to simulate either horizontal or vertical travel.

In this example, an image of a plane travels from right to left across the LEDs. The example also includes the use of loops to repeat an action a number of times.

As discussed in Chapter 6, it may be helpful to sketch the image on paper to show the relevant LEDs to be illuminated, as shown below.

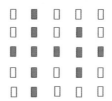

This chapter draws on ideas in the BBC micro:bit MicroPython Documentation, copyright multiple authors, including Damien P. George and Nicholas H. Tollervey.

Coding the Movement of the Plane

Six images must be coded to show the movement of the plane from right to left, starting from a full view and finishing with the plane out of sight.

As stated in Chapter 6, the images are coded as a matrix of 9's and 0's. 9 illuminates an LED at maximum brightness, i.e. fully On, while 0 represents an LED which is Off. The numbers 1 to 8 inclusive can be used to display the LEDs with varying levels of brightness.

So the plane shown on the previous page, in its initial full view position, could be coded as shown on the right below. The corresponding illuminated LEDs are shown on the left.

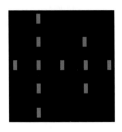

```
plane1 = Image("09000:"
             "09090:"
             "99999:"
             "09090:"
             "09000")
```

To make the plane start to "fly" (or perhaps "taxi") from right to left, we need to produce 5 more images. This is done by successively deleting the left-hand column of LEDs and adding a column of 0's on the right. This is done 5 times until the matrix consists entirely of 0's, i.e. the plane has disappeared.

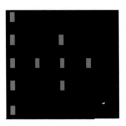

```
plane2 = Image("90000:"
             "90900:"
             "99990:"
             "90900:"
             "90000")
```

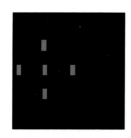

```
plane3 = Image("00000:"
               "09000:"
               "99900:"
               "09000:"
               "00000")
```

```
plane4 = Image("00000:"
               "90000:"
               "99000:"
               "90000:"
               "00000")
```

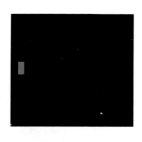

```
plane5 = Image("00000:"
               "00000:"
               "90000:"
               "00000:"
               "00000")
```

```
plane6 = Image("00000:"
               "00000:"
               "00000:"
               "00000:"
               "00000")
```

Coding the micro:bit LEDs in a Single Line

The coding for the plane used so far corresponds to the layout of the 5 x 5 matrix of LEDs on the BBC micro:bit, as shown below.

```
plane1 = Image("09000:"
              "09090:"
              "99999:"
              "09090:"
              "09000")
```

However, the image can be coded in a single line as shown below.

```
plane1= Image("09000:09090:99999:09090:09000")
```

Please note in the above:
- plane1 is a variable name which we make up.
- Image is coded with a capital I.
- Reading from left to right in the single line of coding above, each block of 5 digits represents a row of the 5 x 5 grid of LEDs on the micro:bit, starting from the top row.
- Please also note the use of the brackets, colons (:) and speech marks.
- A single mistake in the syntax above will prevent the program from working.

The above single line layout is used in the rest of this section, for plane1 to plane6 inclusive, as shown on the next page.

Programming the Plane

Shown below is a program to move the plane across the LEDs on the micro:bit from right to left.

```
1  from microbit  import *
2
3  plane1 = Image("09000:09090:99999:09090:09000")
4  plane2 = Image("90000:90900:99990:90900:90000")
5  plane3 = Image("00000:09000:99900:09000:00000")
6  plane4 = Image("00000:90000:99000:90000:00000")
7  plane5 = Image("00000:00000:90000:00000:00000")
8  plane6 = Image("00000:00000:00000:00000:00000")
9
10 display.show(plane1)
11 sleep(10000)
12 display.show(plane2)
13 sleep(200)
14 display.show(plane3)
15 sleep(200)
16 display.show(plane4)
17 sleep(200)
18 display.show(plane5)
19 sleep(200)
20 display.show(plane6)
```

- Line 1 above makes all the MicroPython functions, images, libraries, etc., available to the program. (Continued on the next page.)

- Lines 3-8 assign the rows of LEDs representing the plane in different positions to the variable stores plane1, plane 2, etc.

- Lines 10, 12, 14, 16, 18 and 20 display images of the plane starting off in full view and then travelling from right to left (or perhaps East to West) in stages until it finally disappears.

- Line 11 pauses the full image on the screen for 10 seconds. Subsequent sleep commands pause the images just long enough for them to be seen.

Exercise 7: Running the Plane Program

- Select **New** in the Mu editor and copy the program shown on page 65.

- **Save** the program in a folder on your computer.

- Connect the micro:bit and select the **Flash** button in Mu to copy the program to the micro:bit and run or execute it.

- The image of the plane should be displayed on the LEDs for 10 seconds and then move off.

- If the image is not displayed, check for any errors in the program in Mu before correcting them and flashing and running the program again.

- Experiment with different sleep settings in lines 11, 13, 15, 17 and 19 to try to get the smoothest "flight" of the plane.

Inserting an Infinite Loop

- Insert a new line 9, while True: and make sure the lines below line 9, i.e. 10-20, are *indented by 4 spaces* as shown on the next page.

```
 9   while True:
10       display.show(plane1)
11       sleep(10000)
12       display.show(plane2)
13       sleep(200)
14       display.show(plane3)
15       sleep(200)
16       display.show(plane4)
17       sleep(200)
18       display.show(plane5)
19       sleep(200)
20       display.show(plane6)
```

Block under a while loop indented by 4 spaces → (line 13)

- Flash the modified program to the micro:bit and run it. You should find the while True: statement causes the plane to repeatedly "take off".

  As stated elsewhere in this book, while True: is always true so the program executes the indented lines in an *infinite loop* (or until you unplug the micro:bit).

Inserting a Finite Loop

- To execute the loop a fixed number of times, insert counter=1 and counter = counter+1 statements as discussed on pages 7 and 31-34. Also insert a while condition such as:

  while counter < 5:

  This would display the flight of the plane 4 times.

Exercise 8: Animating Your Own Image

- Think of a vehicle you can move or another object you can animate.

- Design the image using the matrix of 5 x 5 LEDs on the micro:bit.

- Code the image in 5 rows of 5 digits as shown on pages 62 and 63 using 9's to repesent LEDs switched On and 0's for LEDs which are Off. Use digits 1 to 8 inclusive for other levels of brightness.

- Now code 5 more 5 x 5 matrices similar to those on pages 62 and 63 to represent your vehicle or object in different positions as it moves across and leaves the matrix of LEDs.

- Next code your six images in *single line statements*, as shown on pages 64 and 65.

- Enter your images in a program in Mu similar to the program on page 65 to represent the movement of your vehicle or creature, etc.

- **Save** the program and **Flash** and run or execute it.

- If necessary, correct any errors and flash and re-run the program.

- Experiment with different times in the sleep statements to optimise the movement of the object.

- Modify the program using while, etc., as discussed on page 67, to include:

   (a) an infinite loop.

   (b) a loop executed a fixed number of times.

Suggestions for Further Work

You might also like to try using the methods described in this chapter to make:

- A train or another vehicle *approach from the right*, pause while displayed in full, then leave towards the left and disappear.

- A hot air ballon or rocket rise *vertically* into the sky or a boat sink from the surface until out of sight.

A neat solution to the sinking boat is given in the BBC micro:bit MicroPython Documentation, page 9 and shown below. This uses the *list* feature in Python, (discussed in the next chapter) to store and display all of the images of the boat. A list uses *square brackets*, as shown below.

```
all_boats=[boat1, boat2, boat3, boat4, boat5, boat6]
display.show(all_boats, delay=200)
```

A Sinking Boat

(Copyright 2015-2016. BBC micro:bit MicroPython Documentation. Multiple authors).

Summary

- The 5 x 5 LEDs on the BBC micro:bit can be coded to represent an image such as a plane, helicopter or boat, etc., using 5 rows of 5 digits from 0 to 9 inclusive, as discussed in Chapter 6.

- Horizontal or vertical movement of the image can be simulated by creating 6 separate images representing the object, starting from full view and disappearing in stages.

- *Animation* is achieved by displaying each image in turn, using a suitable sleep or delay command between views to adjust the speed of travel.

- Coding of each image can be compacted into a *single line of code* for each image, with a *variable name* such as plane1, etc.

- It's very easy to make a mistake which will stop a program from running. Typical mistakes are a missed bracket, unbalanced speech marks or a misspelt *Python keyword* such as impart instead of import.

- It's also very easy to correct mistakes in the Mu editor, then flash the program again, repeating this process until the program is correct.

- As mentioned on the previous page and discussed in more detail in the next chapter, the *list* feature is used to store a large number of objects (within square brackets) and *iterate* over them in a loop.

8

Lists and Loops

Introduction

Previous chapters have shown how the while loop can be used to repeat the indented block of lines which follows the while statement and colon(:). The while loop is repeated or *iterated* a number of times, until something is no longer true or some condition is not met. Alternatively a loop can be repeated indefinitely using while True:, a statement which is always true.

This chapter looks at some more important features and functions in MicroPython which can be used to program and control the BBC micro:bit. The same Python programming features are used in commerce and industry, and include:

- *Lists* of data items — objects such as names, words, numbers or a mixture of these. Lists can easily be processed in a loop.

- Further looping using for and the range() function.

- *Nested* loops i.e. loops within loops.

- The random module in MicroPython, which, for example, can be used to select random numbers for a game or pick random items out of a list.

- Using the str() function to convert *integers* (whole numbers) to *strings*, which are acceptable to the MicroPython display command, (unlike integers).

Lists in Python and MicroPython

A list allows you to assign multiple pieces of data to a single *variable name*, such as Our_Cats shown below. The list is enclosed in *square brackets* and the items of data are separated by commas, as shown below.

Our_Cats = ["Serena", "Coco", "Halebop", "Meadow"]

The capital letters and underscore in the variable name Our_Cats are optional, but may be included to improve readability. In the above example, all of the items of data are text, i.e. letters, known as *strings* and enclosed within speech marks. *Numbers*, as used in counting and calculations, rather than the *characters* themselves, are not enclosed in speech marks.

A list can also include a mixture of strings and numbers, as shown below:

scores = ["Sue", 24, "Tom", 29, "Ann", 17, "Mike", 18]

The for Loop

All of the items in a list, such as Our_Cats shown above, can be displayed using a for loop, as shown on the next page. cat shown on page 73 is a *variable name* which you make up to hold each individual cat's name in turn as the program iterates around the for loop. So cat would first contain "Serina", then "Coco", then "Halebop", then "Meadow". Instead of cat you could use any variable name you like (apart from MicroPython reserved words).

Note the colon (:) at the end of the for statement in line 5 and the indentation of 4 spaces before the display statement in line 6.

| Indented
4 spaces | for cat in Our_Cats:
    display.scroll(cat) | for **loop** |

The above loop takes the first item in the list and scrolls it on the LED matrix on the BBC micro:bit. Then it moves on to the next item in the list and scrolls that on the LEDs. This process is repeated until all of the items have been scrolled. In this example, only a single display line is repeated in the for loop, rather than a large *indented block of statements* as used in some loops. Each *pass* around the loop is also known as an *iteration*.

The previous statements are shown below in a program which iterates through the list of cats and scrolls each of their names once on the 5 x 5 matrix of LEDs on the micro:bit.

```
1   from microbit import *
2
3   Our_Cats = ["Serena", "Coco", "Halebop", "Meadow"]
4
5   for cat in Our_Cats:
6       display.scroll(cat)
```

Lists can be much bigger than the example above. Together with the for loop, this makes it very easy to process large quantities of data in a short time.

Nested Loops

To keep repeating the scrolling of the cats' names, the for loop near the bottom of page 73 could itself be *nested* within a while True: loop, as shown below.

Note that the for statement, shown below, is indented by 4 spaces under the while True: statement. The display command in the for loop is indented by a further 4 spaces.

In the example below, instead of being nested within the never ending while True: loop, you could specify a fixed number of passes around a for loop as discussed shortly.

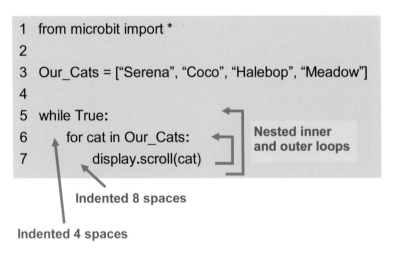

```
1  from microbit import *
2
3  Our_Cats = ["Serena", "Coco", "Halebop", "Meadow"]
4
5  while True:
6      for cat in Our_Cats:
7          display.scroll(cat)
```

Nested inner and outer loops

Indented 8 spaces

Indented 4 spaces

Indentation

After a colon at the end of a line, as in a while statement or in a for statement, Python automatically indents the next line or block of lines by 4 spaces. When loops are *nested*, the block of lines under each extra while or for statement must be indented by a further 4 spaces. So with a total of 3 loops, say, the inner block will be indented 12 spaces.

Putting the Plane in a Loop

On pages 62-65, the images of a plane in different positions were assigned to the variable names, plane1, plane2, etc., as shown on page 65.

These can be put in a list, such as:

```
all_planes = [plane1, plane2, plane3, plane4, plane5, plane6]
```

Variable names such as plane1, plane2, etc., are not enclosed in speech marks in lists, as is the case with *string data*, such as "Jack" or "Jill".

Now to display each image in turn we can use the for loop described on the previous page. This program will use lines 1-9 of the program shown on page 65.

```
10   all_planes = [plane1, plane2, plane3, plane4, plane5,
11   plane6]
12   for plane in all_planes:
13         display.show(plane)
14         sleep(200)
```

Looping the Loop

To display the plane continuously we can add while True: before the for loop shown above. Note that the whole of the for loop must be *nested*, i.e. indented, within the while True: loop as shown below.

```
12   while True:
13         for plane in all_planes:
14               display.show(plane)
15               sleep(200)
```

A very concise way of animating the plane using a list is shown below, replacing lines 12-15 on the previous page.

```
12 display.show(all_planes, loop=True, delay=200)
```

- display.show iterates through the all-planes list and displays the images one at a time.
- loop=True replaces while True: to create an infinite loop, displaying the plane repeatedly.
- delay=200 pauses the display by a fifth of a second.

The above code is based on the sinking boat example given on page 9 of the BBC micro:bit MicroPython Documentation, Copyright 2015-2016, Multiple Authors.

Exercise 9: Coding a List

- Make up a list of your own, similar to Our_Cats on page 72.
- Write a program using a for loop and display.scroll to scroll all of the items in the list across the LEDs on the micro:bit.
- *Nest* or enclose the for loop within a while True: loop to display the list repeatedly.
- *Nest* the for loop within a while < n: loop. E.g. if n is 6 the list will be displayed 5 times.
- Use a *list* to code the movement of an object such as a plane or hot air balloon mentioned earlier. Make the object move across the LEDs on the micro:bit horizontally or vertically.
- Use *nesting* to enclose the for loop within a while loop to repeat the movement of the object either continually or a fixed number of times.
- Use a single display.show command as shown at the top of this page to animate the object.

The **range()** Function

This function allows you to repeat a for loop a specified number of times. For example, to scroll the previous list of cats names across the LEDs a total of 3 times, we could use the following code.

```
1   from microbit import *
2
3   Our_Cats = ["Serena", "Coco", "Halebop", "Meadow"]
4
5   for number in range(3):
6           for cat in Our_Cats:
7                   display.scroll(cat)
```

number and cat above are variable names which you make up.

The range() function can have up to 3 *arguments* (or numbers in the brackets). For example:

range(1, 11, 2)

This means the numbers from 1 up to 11 (but not including 11 itself) ascending in *steps* of 2, i.e.

1, 3, 5, 7, 9

An extra step is needed when working with numbers on the micro:bit. The display.show and display.scroll commands expect *strings*, i.e. letters or *characters*, not mathematical or counting numbers. So numbers need to be converted to strings for display on the micro:bit, using the str() function, discussed on the next page.

The str() Function

This is used for converting a number to a string of characters which can be scrolled across the 5 x 5 matrix of LEDs on the micro:bit. Each number must be placed in brackets, as shown below:

str(number)

In the line above, str is the name of the Python function which converts numbers to strings. number can be any variable name which you choose to represent the *argument*, i.e. the contents of the brackets.

The number is supplied by the range() function, as shown below.

The following short example scrolls all the numbers from 0 to 100, in steps of 5.

```
1   from microbit import *
2
3   for number in range(0,101,5):
4       display.scroll(str(number))
5       sleep(500)
```

This displays the numbers 0, 5, 10, ...95, 100. (If 100 was used instead of 101 in line 3 of the code above, the display would stop at 95).

Exercise 10: Using range() and string()

Write a program to display on the BBC micro:bit all the numbers from 0 to 1000 in steps of 25. (Make sure that 1000, not 975, is the last number displayed).

The random Module

Some *functions* in Python (and MicroPython) are *built in* and can be used by simply including their name directly in a program. Two such built-in functions are range() and str() just discussed on pages 77 and 78.

A *module* is a .py file in the Python library which contains a number of functions. For example, the math module contains many functions such as math.sqrt() for calculating square roots. The random module contains several functions such as random.randint() and random.choice() discussed below.

True random numbers are generated by pure chance, without any method or deliberate choice. Random numbers produced by a computer are said to be *pseudo random*, i.e. not truly random, since they are generated by a program.

random.randint(x, y)

This produces a random number between the integers, i.e. whole numbers, x and y inclusive. This could be used to simulate, say, 20 rolls of a dice as follows:

```
1   from microbit import *
2
3   import random
4
5   for roll in range(20):
6       display.scroll(str(random.randint(1,6)))
7       sleep(500)
```

The above program is explained on the next page, apart from the now very familiar line 1, which makes all of the MicroPython pre-written code available to the program.

```
3   import random
```

Imports the random module of pre-written functions from the Python Library, such as random.randint shown below.

```
5   for roll in range(20):
```

This repeats the block of lines which follow the semicolon, a total of 20 times. roll is a variable name chosen by the user to represent the 20 rolls of the dice and takes the values 0 to 19 inclusive.

```
6        display.scroll(str(random.randint(1,6)))
```

Scrolls across the LEDs on the micro:bit, *random integers*, i.e. whole numbers, from 1 to 6 inclusive. The for loop at line 5 causes this to happen 20 times. display.scroll works better than display.show in this example.

```
7        sleep(500)
```

This pauses the display for half a second (500 milliseconds) to allow each number to be viewed.

Output

The output on the LEDs from one particular execution of this program was as follows:

```
4 5 3 6 4 6 1 3 1 2 5 3 1 3 4 3 6 1 2 5
```

Results after "rolling" a dice 20 times

To display the number of each roll of the dice (from 0 to 19 inclusive in this example), add line 8 to the program on page 79, indented as shown below.

```
8        display.scroll(str(roll))
```

random.choice()

The following program can be used to pick a name or item at random from a list (i.e. in square brackets). range(5) means the for loop will be executed a total of 5 times.

```
1   from microbit import *
2
3   import random
4
5   friends=["Jill", "Jim", " Carol", "Mike", "Sam"]
6
7   for winner in range(5):
6       display.scroll(random.choice(friends))
```

The output from one execution of this program was:

Mike Jill Carol Mike Jim

Exercise 11: The **random** Module

- Write a program to scroll random numbers between 1 and 10 inclusive across the LEDs on the micro:bit. Use range() to make this happen a total of 6 times.

- Execute the program several times using the *program reset button* on the back of the micro:bit, as shown on page 4. Note the results and decide if you think the results are truly random.

- Write a program which includes the signs of the Zodiac in a *list*. Use random.choice() to select a star sign and display it on the micro:bit. Use the range() function to repeat the display a total of 5 times.

Summary

- A large number of items can be placed in a *list* within *square brackets*, separated by commas.

- Text such as names of people in a list must be placed in speech marks, unlike mathematical numbers and variable names, such as plane1, etc.

- A list can be processed, e.g. displayed, in a for loop which *iterates* over each invidual item in turn.

- A loop may be *nested* within another loop such as a for loop within a while loop. The inner loop is completed first and this is repeated a number of times until the outer loop is completed.

- Blocks of code under a while or for loop are indented by 4 spaces. Blocks of code in a nested (inner) loop must be indented by a further 4 spaces.

- The range() function can be used to specify the number of times a for loop *iterates* through a list.

- range(x, y, z) can be used to generate a series of numbers starting at x, finishing at y, in steps of z.

- A Python *module* is a *.py file* containing various *functions*. e.g. math.cos(x) in the math module. A module must be *imported*, as in import random.

- The random module provides the function randint() to select a random *integer* from a range of numbers, e.g. random.randint(1,6).

- The function random.choice() is used to select a name, string or number at random from a list.

- The str() function is used to convert *integers* to *strings* for use in the display command.

Music and Sounds

Introduction

This chapter looks at:

- Connecting headphones or speakers to the BBC micro:bit.

- Using the micro:bit to play music and sounds from the MicroPython *music module*.

- Using *lists* and *loops* to play music and sounds *sequentially* or at *random*.

- Composing your own music and sounds.

- Using the MicroPython *speech synthesiser* to type in words for the micro:bit to say aloud in a voice which can be adjusted.

Inexpensive audio cables, as shown below, are available from companies such as Kitronik, Farnell, Maplin and Amazon. The red crocodile clip connects to **Pin 0** on the micro:bit while the black one is connected to the **GND** pin, as shown on the next page. The other end of the audio cable has a *3.5mm jack* (socket) to accept the cable from your headphones or speaker.

3.5mm
audio jack

crocodile
clips

micro:bit audio cable

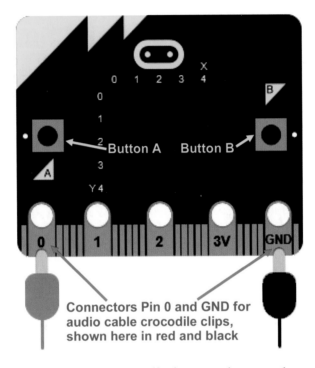

Connectors Pin 0 and GND for
audio cable crocodile clips,
shown here in red and black

Instead of headphones, small, inexpensive speakers are available, such as the **micro:bit Mini-speaker**, from the **micro:bit accessories** Website and from Amazon.

micro:bit
Mini-speaker

The music Module

Chapters 6 and 7 showed how you can display the collection of pre-written images built into MicroPython, before starting to create your own. Similarly you can easily play pre-written music and sounds from the MicroPython music module, before developing your own music.

The built-in music and sounds are as follows:

music.DADADADUM	music.PUNCHLINE
music.ENTERTAINER	music.PYTHON
music.PRELUDE	music.BADDY
music.ODE	music.CHASE
music.NYAN	music.BA_DING
music.RINGTONE	music.WAWAWAWAA
music.FUNK	music.JUMP_UP
music.BLUES	music.JUMP_DOWN
music.BIRTHDAY	music.POWER_UP
music.WEDDING	music.POWER_DOWN
music.FUNERAL	

Each of the above can be played using the music.play statement shown on the next page.

The micro:bit should be connected to your computer and your headphones or speakers connected to the micro:bit, as discussed on page 83. A program to play an individual tune, such as PYTHON, selected from the list shown on the previous page, would be as follows:

```
1 from microbit import *
2
3 import music
4
5 music.play(music.PYTHON)
```

In the above program, import music is needed to give the program access to all of the pre-written music and sounds in the MicroPython music module. Please also note the use of capital letters for the name of the piece of music.

Non-stop Music

To keep playing a piece of music continuously, insert while True: before the music.play statement, as shown below.

```
1 from microbit import *
2
3 import music
4
5 while True:
6     music.play(music.PYTHON)
```

Please note the colon (:) on line 5, the indentation on line 6, and the captal letters in True: and PYTHON.

MicroPython Medleys

Chapter 8 discussed the *list* feature in Python, in which a number of items are enclosed in square brackets and separated by commas.

Such a list allows the items to be processed and displayed in various ways. For example, we can put all of the pieces of music and sounds from the music module into a list. Then play all of the pieces in a continuous medley, one after the other, i.e. *sequentially*.

Alternatively we can use the random module in Python to select a piece of music or a sound at random from the list and then play it. Then using an infinite while True: loop, keep selecting and playing random tunes continuously. Coding for these medleys is shown below.

Playing the List of Tunes Sequentially

The program below uses a for loop to *iterate*, i.e. repeatedly work through, the list of tunes, playing them one after the other.

```
1  from microbit import *
2
3  import music
4
5  playlist = [music.PRELUDE, music.ODE,
6  music.NYAN, music.FUNK, music.BIRTHDAY,
7  music.PYTHON, music.BADDY, music.CHASE]
8
9  for tune in playlist:
10      music.play(tune)
```

Please note in the program on the previous page:

- playlist is any name (preferably meaningful) made up by the programmer/coder. medley or tunes, for example, might equally be used.

- The list of tunes starting on line 5 is only a sample from the complete list in the MicroPython music module, due to limitations of the printed page. However, the complete list of tunes shown on page 85 of this book can easily be entered into the Mu editor.

- To keep the whole of each line of code visible in the Mu editor, press **Return** or **Enter** when reaching the right-hand edge of the screen. Then carry on entering the names of the tunes and sounds on the next line.

- In the for loop shown below and on page 87, tune in both lines 9 and 10 is any relevant name made up by the programmer. melody or jingle, for example, could be used instead of tune.

```
8
9  for tune in playlist:
10     music.play(tune)
```

- The for loop plays the first tune in the list and then passes through the list playing each of the tunes in sequence until all of the tunes have been played.

- To keep playing the list repeatedly, enter while True: at line 8, making sure line 9 is then indented by 4 spaces and line 10 is indented by a total of 8 spaces.

Playing Tunes at Random

The program for playing the tunes at random is shown below:

```
1  from microbit import *
2
3  import music
4
5  import random
6
7  jingles = [music.PRELUDE, music.ODE,
8  music.NYAN, music.FUNK, music.BIRTHDAY,
9  music.PYTHON, music.BADDY, music.CHASE ]
10
11 while True:
12     music.play(random.choice(jingles))
```

This is similar to the program on page 87, except:

- We need to import the Python random module at line 5. This contains the random.choice function needed to select items randomly from a list.

- The program passes repeatedly around the infinite while True: loop, playing tunes at random, non-stop unless you unplug the micro:bit.

- Line 12 is saying "play a tune at random from the list of tunes which has been assigned the name jingles."

Mistakes which I find particularly easy to make include missing off the last square bracket, missing the colon (:) in while True: and not balancing the *parentheses* (i.e. round brackets in plain English) in line 12.

Exercise 12: Playing Tunes

- Open the Mu editor and select **New**.

- Copy the program at the bottom of page 87. Enter all of the tunes and sounds listed on page 85, not just the small sample shown on page 87, pressing **Enter/ Return** at the end of each line on the Mu screen.

- **Save** the program in a folder of your choice on your computer, with a meaningful file name. Connect the micro:bit and your headphones or speaker, as described on pages 83 and 84.

- Select **Flash** to copy the program to the micro:bit and start playing the tunes in sequence.

- Make a note of your 5 favourite tunes. If necessary you can play all the tunes again by pressing the **Program reset button** shown on page 4.

Now edit the program as follows:

- Change **playlist** to a meaningful name of your own choice, wherever it occurs in the program.

- Edit the list to include only your 5 favourite tunes.

- Change **tune** to a meaningful name of your own choice, wherever it occurs in the program.

- Select **Save** then **Flash** to start playing your 5 favourite tunes in *sequence*.

Modify the program, as discussed on page 89, to:

- import the random module.

- Replace the for loop with a while True: loop.

- Include the random.choice function, as shown on page 89, line 12 but with your own list name, instead of jingles.

- Select **Save** then **Flash** to start playing your favourite tunes in *random* order.

Creating Your Own Music

MicroPython uses the letters A to G to represent notes in the following format:

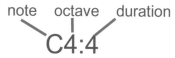

The octaves specify how high or low a note will be played, with 0 being the lowest note and 8 the highest. A piece of music is coded in a *list* with square brackets as follows:

```
1  from microbit import *
2  import music
3
4  tune=["C4:4", "A", "G", "E", "F", "G", "E", "C", "C",
5  "A", "G", "E", "F", "G", "D"]
6
7  music.play(tune)
```

In a series of notes with the same octave and duration, only the first note needs to be fully defined, as in "C4:4" in line 4 above. To code a *silence*, include the letter R as a note in the list and include a duration, such as R:4, for example.

Exercise 13: Creating Tunes

- Copy the above program into the Mu editor and save it as a .py file with a meaningful name.

- Connect the micro:bit and headphones or speaker then flash and run the code to play the simple tune.

- Now create your own tune in lines 4 and 5 and flash and execute the code. Continue editing and flashing the code until you're satisfied with your new tune.

Speech

MicroPython has a *speech module* which allows you to type in words for the micro:bit to speak. To use the speech module you will need to have your headphones or speaker connected to the micro:bit and the micro:bit connected to your computer, as discussed on pages 83 and 84. For speech synthesis, the crocodile clips should be connected to **Pins 0** and **1** as shown below. It doesn't matter which connector, red or black, is connected to which pin.

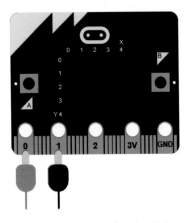

When writing a speech program in the Mu editor, first you need to import the MicroPython speech module. The code to speak the traditional computing greeting "Hello, World" is shown below.

```
import speech
speech.say("Hello, World")
```

The MicroPython speech synthesiser allows you to modify the voice using four parameters, each in the range 0-255. The parameters are shown on the next page.

- **Pitch**: How high the voice is.
- **Speed**: How fast the words are spoken.
- **Mouth**: How clearly the words are pronounced.
- **Throat**: How relaxed the voice is.

The following code, including the well-known saying from Doctor Who, is quoted from the BBC micro:bit MicroPython Documentation:

```
1  from microbit import *
2
3   import speech
4
5  speech.say ("I am a DALEK — EXTERMINATE",
6  speed=120, pitch=100, throat=100, mouth=200)
```

Exercise 14: Making a Speech

- Copy the above code into the Mu editor and **Save** it as a .py file with a meaningful name.
- With the micro:bit and headphones or speaker connected to your computer, **Flash** the code and check that it runs correctly.
- Alter line 5 and 6 to a speech of your choice or a favourite line from a poem, song or catchphrase.
- Experiment with different values of speed, pitch, throat and mouth using values from 0 to 255 to obtain the voice which you like best.

Please note that in the above short program, line 1 is not essential, but it will normally be needed in larger programs so its use in programs as a general rule is recommended.

Summary

- MicroPython has a music module containing pre-written melodies and sounds. The statement import music makes the module available to a program.

- To play music (and sounds), it's necessary to connect headphones or a speaker to **Pin 0** and **Pin GND** on the micro:bit, via an audio cable.

- Music and sounds from the module are coded in the format music.PYTHON and played using a statement, such as music.play(music.PYTHON) to play the theme music from the television series.

- Pieces of music such as music.PYTHON and music.BIRTHDAY, etc., can be placed in a playlist, using the Python *list* feature, with square brackets and the tunes separated by commas.

- A for loop can be used to *iterate* through the list and play all of the tunes and sounds in *sequence*.

- A while True: loop can be used together with the random.choice function to continually play tunes selected randomly.

- Your own tunes can be created using a list of letters and numbers such as B5:4, where B is the *note*, 5 is the *octave* and 4 is the *duration*. Letters A-G can be used for the note and numbers 0-8 for both the octave and the duration.

- The import speech statement enables you to type in words for the micro:bit to speak using the speech.say command. Parameters speed, pitch, throat and mouth allow the voice to be modified to your liking.

Branching and Movement

Introduction

A built-in *accelerometer* detects, measures and displays any movements and gestures when the BBC micro:bit is moved. Similarly an onboard *compass* displays the direction in which the micro:bit is pointing.

Branching

The accelerometer is described shortly, but first it may be helpful to discuss some important Python statements which will be used with the accelerometer and are also used in many other Python programs. These statements are if, elif and else. (elif is short for else if). They are known as *branching* because they can cause program execution to be diverted, out of sequence, to alternative statements. This depends on whether statements are true or false or if certain *events* happen or don't happen. The statements are often used in groups of 3, although it's possible to have more than one elif statement. A large program might have several groups of if, elif and else statements. These statements work in the following way:

- if this statement is true carry out the block of indented statements which follow the colon (:). Otherwise move on down to the next statement.

- elif this statement is true carry out the next indented block of statements. Otherwise move on down.

- else if none of the above statements are true, execute the following block of indented statements.

The three Python keywords, if, elif and else can also be used to determine what a program does when something happens, such as the pressing of button **A** or button **B** on the front of the micro:bit, as shown on pages 3 and 84.

The program below uses the while True: infinite loop to keep repeating the block of lines which follows, since while True: is always true, as previously stated.

```
1   from microbit import *
2
3   import music
4
5   while True:
6
7       if button_a.is_pressed():
8           music.play(music.BIRTHDAY)
9
10      elif button_b.is_pressed():
11          break
12
13      else:
14          music.play(music.WEDDING)
```

Please note above and below, the buttons on the micro:bit are coded as button_a and button_b. The code .is_pressed(): makes line 7 True if button **A** is pressed. Line 10 works in a similar way for button **B**.

```
7       if button_a.is_pressed():
```

The Program in Detail

- from microbit import * is the ever present statement to make all of the code for the microbit hardware available to this program.

- import music means "make all the tunes in the MicroPython music module, as shown on page 85, available to this program."

- On each pass through the while True: loop, if you don't press either of the buttons **A** or **B** on the micro:bit, lines 7, 8, 10 and 11 are ignored, since lines 7 and 10 are not True.

- Program execution passes to line 13, the else statement. This causes line 14 to be executed and the WEDDING tune is played.

- The program continues round the loop and if buttons **A** or **B** are still not pressed, the WEDDING tune is repeatedly played.

- The program can be stopped by pressing button **B** to execute the break statement to exit the loop.

- If you press button **A** at any time, the BIRTHDAY tune is played once before reverting to the WEDDING tune, which is played non-stop in the endless loop unless a button is pressed.

- If you keep button **A** held down, the BIRTHDAY tune is played continuously until button **A** is released and the WEDDING tune is again played continuously.

break

The break statement, line 11 in this small example, exits the while True: loop and ends the program. In a large program the break statement would cause the program to leave the loop and continue downwards to execute the next (unindented) statement after the loop.

Exercise 15: Using the Buttons

- Open a **New** program in Mu and copy then **Save** the program shown on page 96.

- Connect the micro:bit and headphones or speaker to your computer and **Flash** the program to execute it.

- Experiment by firstly not pressing any buttons while the program is running.

- Then press button **A** just once and see what happens.

- Now hold down button **A** continuously.

- Finally press button **B**.

- If the micro:bit doesn't play the **BIRTHDAY** or **WEDDING** tunes or break out of the loop, as discussed on page 97, check for errors in the Mu code or error messages scrolled across the LEDs on the micro:bit.

- If necessary, correct any errors and **Flash** the program to the micro:bit. Repeat until the program is correct.

- Now edit lines 7 and 10 to play two completely different tunes chosen from the list on page 85. Repeat the testing shown above.

- Next repeat the program using 2 *images* not tunes. Change line 8 and line 14 so that each uses the display.show command (page 17) to display an image chosen from the MicroPython image library. These images can all be viewed on the Web as described on page 51, but in the meantime you could choose two images from the following :

Image.HAPPY	Image.SAD
Image.ANGRY	Image.SILLY
Image.SMILE	Images.ASLEEP

The Accelerometer

An accelerometer measures *changes in speed*. When a car driver presses down on the *accelerator*, the car increases in speed and passengers may feel a *force* from their seat.

There is also the *acceleration* due to gravity, the force which attracts a body towards the centre of the earth, such as a cat falling out of a tree. The acceleration due to gravity is known a *1g* and is quoted as 32ft/sec/sec or 9.8m/sec/sec.

Accelerometers have many important applications, such as:

- Assisting in the navigation of ships and aircraft.
- Detecting a sudden change in the speed of a car and inflating the airbags before a collision.
- Rotating the screen display on a phone as required.
- Switching off a hard disc drive to prevent damage when a laptop computer is dropped.
- Switching off a device such as an electric fire, etc., if it's knocked over.

The BBC micro:bit has an on-board accelerometer on a small chip as highlighted in red below.

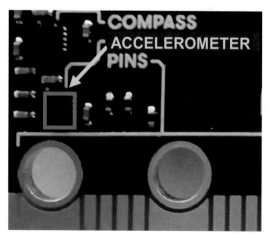

Using the Accelerometer

The accelerometer measures movement along 3 axes, i.e. **x**, (left to right), **y** (forward and back) and **z** (up and down).

The unit of measurements is the *milli-g* where 1g is 1024 milli-gs or the acceleration due to gravity.

When you move or tilt the micro:bit, the acceleration along the 3 axes can be detected by the following statements:

```
x= accelerometer.get_x()
y = accelerometer.get_y()
z = accelerometer.get_z()
```

We can connect the micro:bit to the computer, move it about and display its accelerations in all 3 directions.

Exercise 16: Measuring Acceleration

- With the micro:bit connected to your computer select **Repl** shown on page 101 to display the lower panel.

- Select **New** and enter and **Save** the program shown on page 101. Then **Flash** it to the micro:bit.

- Now tilt the micro:bit along the **x** axis, up and down on the left and right repeatedly.

- The print statement in line 5 displays the accelerations as *output* as shown in the lower panel on page 101.

- Now modify the program to measure the accelerations when the microbit is tilted forwards and backwards in the **y** direction and note the results.

- Modify the program again to measure the acceleration up an down in the **z** direction and note the results.

(The REPL panel should be displayed before flashing. To clear results from the lower panel, click **Repl** twice.)

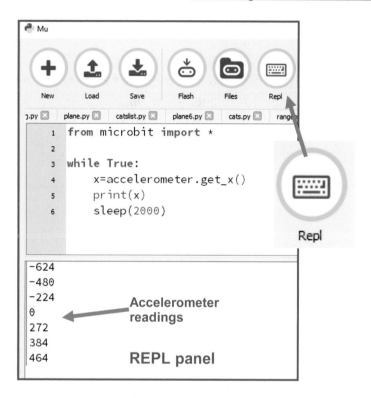

```
1   from microbit import *
2
3   while True:
4       x=accelerometer.get_x()
5       print(x)
6       sleep(2000)
```

Repl

-624
-480
-224
0
272
384
464

Accelerometer readings

REPL panel

Results from Moving the micro:bit

The accelerations range from −1024 to +1024 milli-gs, (-1g to +1g) while 0 is recorded in the **x** and **y** directions when the microbit is stationary on a table. With the LEDs uppermost and the connectors towards you, positive accelerations are obtained from tilting down on the right and down on the front. Negative results occur when the micro:bit is tilted down on the left and down on the back.

In the **z** direction, negative accelerations of about -1g are recorded when resting on a table with the LEDs uppermost. Turn the micro:bit over and positive accelerations of about + 1g are displayed on the REPL panel, shown above.

Gestures

There is a set of *gestures* or movements of the micro:bit which can be detected by MicroPython. If the micro:bit is moved using one of the gestures, this can be coded to cause a particular statement to be executed, as discussed below.

The gestures or movements of the micro:bit have the following names:

up	down	left	right	face up	
face down	freefall	3g	6g	8g	shake

(Fighter pilots and Formula 1 racing drivers can experience forces/accelerations equivalent to 5g or more).

There are several statements for detecting the above movements of the micro:bit, including the following:

```
if accelerometer.was_gesture(name):
```

The statement above checks to see if the named gesture has just been used and if this is true, carries out the next indented statement. If the statement is false, the execution continues to the next statement in the program, i.e. elif.

Syntax

The name of the gesture must be enclosed in speech marks, as shown in "face up" below. Please also note the full stop, underscore (_) and the colon (:).

```
if accelerometer.was_gesture("face up"):
```

The program on the next page detects whether the accelerometer has been face up (i.e. with the 5x5 matrix of LEDs on top) or face down, (i.e. the LEDs underneath). It can also check if the micro:bit is in freefall.

Exercise 17: Detecting Gestures

- With the micro:bit connected copy the program below and **Flash** it as previously described.

```
1  from microbit import *
2
3  while True:
4      if accelerometer.was_gesture("face up"):
5          display.scroll("Things are looking up")
6
7      elif accelerometer.was_gesture("face down"):
8          display.scroll("Can't see a thing")
9
10     elif accelerometer.was_gesture("freefall"):
11         display.scroll("Please help me!")
```

- Place the micro:bit on a table with the LEDs on top. The message "**Things are looking up**" should be scrolled.

- Turn the micro:bit over and "**Can't see a thing**" should be scrolled across the LEDs.

- Now let the micro:bit fall sharply a few feet (onto a soft, cushioned, landing surface) and check that "**Please help me!**" is scrolled.

- Keep repeating the gestures and the 3 messages should continue to be displayed.

- Rewrite the program with 3 different gestures, as listed on page 102, and code 3 messages of your own.

- Test the program with your 3 gestures and make sure they continue to display your messages. Otherwise correct any errors and try again.

Summary

- if, elif and else statements are used to execute alternative statements when certain *conditions* are True or False. Also when specified *events* take place, such as button **A** or button **B** on the micro:bit being pressed, or certain *gestures* or movements are applied to the micro:bit.

- The break statement causes program execution to exit a while True: or for loop and continue down to the next statement.

- The micro:bit has an onboard *accelerometer* which can detect movement along 3 axes **x**, **y** and **z**. (Tilting left and right, tilting forward and back and moving up and down, respectively).

- Acceleration is measured in milli-gs, where 1024 milli-gs or 1g is the acceleration due to gravity. The results of moving the micro:bit along any of the 3 axes can be displayed on the REPL panel in Mu.

- MicroPython includes a set of named gestures such as shake, freefall, face up and face down.

- The accelerometer can detect when these gestures are applied to the micro:bit. The gestures can be used in if, elif and else statements to execute alternative statements, such as scrolling various messages, displaying different images or playing different tunes.

Appendix 1

Bits, Bytes and Hexadecimal

A program written in a language such as Python, based on English words, has to be translated into the computer's *machine code*, which is based on the *binary digits* (or *bits*) 0 and 1. A brief introduction to binary is given below, but first a reminder of our everyday decimal number system.

The Decimal System

The decimal (or *base 10*) number 3,967 is shown below. This has column values of thousands, hundreds, tens and units as shown in the yellow row below.

1000	100	10	1
3	9	6	7

Decimal

The Binary System

In contrast, the binary system has column values based on the number 2, as shown in yellow below. A few random binary numbers are shown in the *nibbles* (groups of 4 bits) below. The equivalent decimal numbers are shown on the right.

8	4	2	1	Decimal
0	0	0	0	0
0	0	0	1	1
0	0	1	0	2
0	1	1	0	6
1	0	1	0	10
1	1	1	1	15

Binary   **Decimal**

Bytes

The binary digits 0 and 1 inside a computer are handled in groups of eight. Each group of bits is known as a *byte* and can be used to represent:

- *Data* such as decimal numbers, letters of the alphabet, punctuation marks, etc.
- *Program instructions* such as to add two numbers.
- *Addresses* of locations in the memory where programs and data are stored.

Data is moved around a computer in wired paths or highways known as *data buses*. Early computers handled data in single bytes and were known as *8-bit* computers. Nowadays *32-bit* and *64-bit* computers are the norm.

The ASCII code

The ASCII code (American Standard Code for Information Interchange) is a list of groups of 8 bits used to represent numbers, letters, punctuation marks, instructions, etc.

So, for example, the letter **A** is represented in the ASCII code by the string of 8 bits shown below:

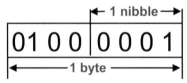

As shown above, a group of 4-bits is known as a *nibble*.

> 1 kilobyte (KB) is 1024 bytes.
> 1 megabyte (MB) is 1024 kilobytes.
> 1 gigabyte (GB) is 1024 megabytes.

Hexadecimal (.hex)

Some advanced programmers need to work in machine code. It would be very time-consuming to write code using bytes or strings each of 8 bits. So the *hexadecimal* (*hex*) code was devised to represent the 4 bits in a nibble by a single character.

As shown below, there are 16 possible combinations of bits in a nibble ranging from 0000 to 1111. The hexadecimal code uses the digits 0-9 and the letters A-F to represent the 16 bit patterns as shown below. So, for example, 0111 is coded as 7 and 1111 is coded as F in hexadecimal.

Decimal	Binary	Hexadecimal
0	0000	0
1	0001	1
2	0010	2
3	0011	3
4	0100	4
5	0101	5
6	0110	6
7	0111	7
8	1000	8
9	1001	9
10	1010	A
11	1011	B
12	1100	C
13	1101	D
14	1110	E
15	1111	F

The ASCII code uses 8 bits to represent numbers, letters, punctuation marks.

So, for example, the letter **C** has the ASCII code shown on the left below:

| 01 0 0 | 0 0 1 1 |

Lettter C in ASCII binary

| 4 | 3 |

Letter C in Hexadecimal

Each nibble of 4 bits has a hexadecimal equivalent as shown in column 3 on the previous page. So the letter **C** would be coded in hex as **43** shown above on the right.

Similarly, the decimal number **255**, would be coded in binary and hexadecimal as shown below.

| 1 1 1 1 | 1 1 1 1 |

255 in ASCII binary

| F | F |

255 in Hexadecimal

So the hexadecimal version of a program is much more compact than the equivalent binary machine code. However, the listing of a program in the hexadecimal code is still difficult for humans to read and understand. Hence the need for *high level* programming languages such as Python, C, Fortran and Pascal, which are based on English words and far removed from the computer's machine code.

Creating a .hex file

Fortunately the compiler in the BBC micro:bit MicroPython editor takes care of the conversion of your Python code to produce a *hexadecimal file* consisting only of digits 0-9 and letters A-F. This file is saved with a *filename* and the extension *.hex*, e.g. *smileyface.hex* and can be run or executed straightaway on the BBC micro:bit.

Levels of Language

Machine code

Machine code, i.e. binary and hexadecimal is classed as the lowest level language and can be directly used by the computer. However, it's very difficult for most humans to understand long strings of 0s and 1s of binary or the numbers and letters of hexadecimal.

High Level Language

These include languages such Python, MicroPython, Pascal, Fortran and C. They are the farthest away from machine code and use English words to make programs easier to write and understand. Examples of *keywords* or *reserved* words in the MicroPython language include while, if, elif, else, import, display, for and sleep.

High level languages are translated to machine code by a compiler or alternatively by an interpreter.

Assembly or Low Level Language

This is between machine code and a high level language. It is easier to understand than machine code but harder to understand than a high level language. Assembly languages are different for different types of computer. They use *mnemonics* to give instructions which refer directly to parts of a computer. For example, in some assembly languages LDA means "Load the Accumulator". (The accumulator is part of the CPU (Central Processing Unit) and stores the answer to a calculation.) Assembly language programs are easy to translate into machine code, using a program called an *assembler*.

The Translation Process

High Level Language

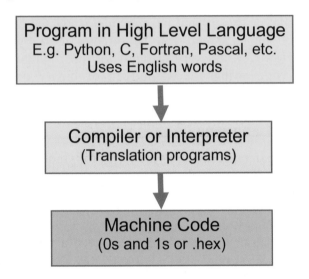

Low Level or Assembly Language

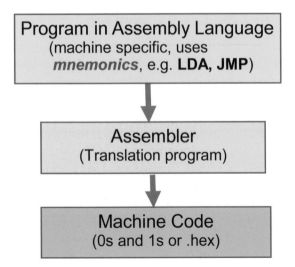

Appendix 2: A Glossary of Terms

Accelerometer

A device that can measure changes in speed on the micro:bit and on aircraft, cars and electrical appliances, etc.

Algorithm

A list of steps needed to complete a process.

ALU (Arithmetic and Logic Unit)

Part of the CPU (Central Processing Unit) in a computer, used for *calculations* and *comparisons*, (e.g. if x > 5, etc.).

Argument

A number or a piece of data being worked on by a *function*. E.g. in the function sqrt(49) the argument is 49.

Assembly Language

A low level programming language between a high level language (such as Python) and machine code. Translated to machine code by an *assembler* program.

Assign

Give a *variable name* to a piece of data, e.g. hours = 37.

Binary

Base 2 number system used at the core of a computer using only the *binary digits* 0 and 1(known as *bits*).

Branching

Switching program execution to alternative statements if certain other statements or *conditions* are *True* or *False.*

Button

Two buttons, **A** and **B**, on the BBC micro:bit can be programmed to execute statements when pressed. A third button is used to *reset* or re-run the current program.

Byte

A group of *8 bits*, used to represent *characters*, *instructions* and *addresses* of memory locations.

Chip

A small piece of silicon, etc., containing electrical circuits and mounted on a board such as the BBC micro:bit.

Code or Source Code

Instructions or *statements* written by a programmer in a language such as Python.

Compiler

A program that translates code in a *high level language* (i.e. *source code*) into an executable version in machine code.

CPU (Central Processing Unit)

A chip or set of chips which carries out or executes the instructions in a program. Also known as a *micropressor*.

Execution

The running of a program, carrying out the instructions.

Flash

Copy code from the Mu editor and run it on the micro:bit.

for

A *loop* which *iterates* through a list of *data* or *range* of numbers carrying out a block of instructions each time.

Function

Process that produces a number as *output* from one or more numbers which are *input*, e.g. sin(60).

Gesture

Movements of the micro:bit, e.g. shake, which can be programmed to execute various statements.

High Level Language (HLL)

A language, such as Python, using English words to write instructions for a computer, translated by a *compiler* or *interpreter* into the computer's own *machine code*.

Indentation

Insetting one or more statements, usually by 4 spaces, to identify a block of statements to be repeated in a loop or executed as alternative statements after if, elif and else.

Input

Data entered into a computer for processing, e.g. from a keyboard, mouse, camera, microphone, USB cable, etc.

Instruction

Line or lines in a program telling a computer what to do.

Interpreter

A program which *translates* and *executes* source code, line by line, without producing a complete machine code version which can be executed later.

Iteration

A *repeated* process such as working through a *list* of items, performing the same process on each item, until the end of the list is reached.

LED Matrix

The array of 5 x 5 Light Emitting Diodes on the micro:bit. Used to display text messages, error messages and images.

Library

Pre-written *functions* and *modules* which can be called up in a program to save coding them from scratch.

List

A sequence of data items separated by *commas* and enclosed in *square brackets*. *Iterable* using a for loop.

Loop

A while statement or a for statement followed by a block of indented lines. The loop is repeated while some condition is True or until a range of numbers has been iterated.

Microcontroller

A small computer on a single *integrated circuit board*, e.g. the BBC micro:bit and the MicroPython *pyboard*. Microcontrollers are used in cars and electrical appliances.

micro:bit

The microcomputer/microcontroller at the centre of the BBC project to help students learn about computers.

Microcomputer

A small computer, e.g. a microcontroller, smartphone, tablet, laptop or desktop. Contains memory (RAM and Read Only), CPU, motherboard, input and output sytems.

Microprocessor

The CPU used in microcomputers. Consists of a single chip on the *motherboard* or *integrated circuit board*.

MicroPython

A version of the Python programming language, created by Damien George for microcontrollers such as the BBC micro:bit and the *pyboard*.

Module

A set of pre-written functions, statements and definitions on a particular subject such as math or random numbers.

Mu

A MicroPython *editor* created by Nicholas Tollervey for writing programs to be *flashed* and *executed* on the BBC micro:bit. Mu includes *REPL* (Read, Evaluate, Print, Loop) which has a *prompt* for writing and testing single lines of code *interactively*, with immediate results.

Nesting

A loop within a loop. The inner loop is executed in its entirety during the first pass around the outer loop. This is repeated for all the subsequent passes around the outer loop.

Operand

A number being worked on or *operated on* in a statement. Can also be an *address* in the memory of a piece of data.

Output

Text, images, sounds, music, etc., produced by a program.

Pin

Connectors on the BBC micro:bit for accessories such as speakers, headphones, robots and other devices.

Program

A set of *statements* or *instructions* executed or run by a computer. Saved in Python as a *.py file*.

RAM (Random Access Memory)

Volatile (temporary) *storage* for current programs and data.

ROM (Read Only Memory) and Flash ROM

ROM is permanent memory used to store systems software. *Flash ROM*, as used in the micro:bit, can be written to but is not lost when the computer is switched off, unlike *RAM*.

Statement

An *instruction* in a high level language such as Python.

String

A set of characters, usually letters or numbers or a mixture of both (an *alphanumeric string*), enclosed in quotes.

Syntax

Rules in the *grammar* of a language such as Python. Syntax errors include incorrect punctuation, unmatched brackets (i.e. not in pairs) and misspelling of *reserved words* in the Python language such as impart instead of import.

True

E.g. the condition "if x is greater than 3 and less than 7" is *true* when x is 4, 5 and 6 and *false* for any other value of x. Used with if, elif and else to execute alternative statements depending on whether or not a conditional statement is true.

while True:

This statement is *always true* and therefore can be used to create an *infinite loop*.

Variable

A name made up by the programmer for a *storage location* to which *numeric* or *string* data is *assigned* e.g.

```
temperature = 27        make = "Porsche"
```

Suggestions for Further Reading

If you've found this introductory guide to Python coding on the BBC micro:bit helpful, you might want to progress to "Programming with MicroPython: Embedded Programming on the Handheld Arm-Powered Computer" from O'Reilly Media, Incorporated. This was written by Nicholas Tollervey, who played a major role in the BBC micro:bit project and created the Mu editor, used throughout this book.

You could also read "Getting Started with the BBC micro:bit" by Mike Tooley, from Bernard Babani (publishing) Ltd, ISBN 978-0-85934-770-9. This includes, amongst many other topics, the Microsoft Block Editor for programming the micro:bit.

The pyboard

Finally, you might like to explore another microcontroller, the *pyboard*, available from the Website **micropython.org**, created by Damien George, who also developed MicroPython and played a major part in the BBC micro:bit project.

Index